Year of

LITTLE LESSON PLANS

10 Minutes of Smart, Fun Things to Teach
Your Little Ones Ages 3-8 Each Weekday

Courtney Loquasto

For Mom.

YEAR of LITTLE LESSON PLANS

Contents

Courtney Loquasto

Education is not preparation for life; education is life itself.

-John Dewey

Courtney Loquasto

Intro: Making Your Little Ones Smarter and More With-It in Just 10 Minutes a Day

How can I keep us talking about smart things?

Hello, Friend - Welcome.

Since you're perusing these pages (thank you for doing that, by the way), I'm assuming you're currently elbows-up in the wild and wonderful experiences that come along with raising young children. Buckle up, right?

I don't know about you, but I've found the experience to be equally as frustrating as it is awesome. Sometimes our days go along just as planned without a hitch. *Most* days contain minor-to-earthshaking special circumstances and distractions, which have a tendency to derail my master plan for the day.   And, as it's gone for the last seven years, it seems educating my kids on everyday stuff suffers first.

Yes, savor those as-planned days! If you're like me, they are few and far-between. Take lots of pictures and post them to Facebook when they happen! That way, you'll have proof that sometimes things do go the way you intended.

This book, however, is for the *rest* of the days - the ones with bee stings, stomach viruses, forgotten lunches, broken dishwashers, dentist appointments, potty-training mishaps, missing naps, knots in shoelaces, nightmares, unexpected visitors, unexplained fevers, class cupcakes and Santa Claus. Oh, and don't forget the postponed trip to the grocery store. That one's a biggie.

And reading this book will help you how, exactly?

Well, this quick-hit guide will assist you in educating and entertaining your little guys and gals, while reminding you of some information you might have – ehem - *misplaced* along the way, in just ten minutes a day.

You'll find a year's worth of weekly themes that match what is actually, legitimately going on in the calendar, and while it's still relevant. You'll soon be able to rattle off refreshingly smart-sounding, interesting things each weekday to your child, without having to lift a finger in the research department.

You might, occasionally need to scrape the crust off the nozzle to your Elmer's, but that's about the extent of any preparation that will be required out of you, because:

What you're holding in your hands is a whole lot of words for your mouth to say.

Yes- even *before* the coffee. Hi-YA morning fog!

Why Bother?

Here's how it happens at our house. See if you can relate with this scenario:

I love the idea of talking to our kids about smart things that are going on in the world. I'll think of something (that I think) is really funny or important while:

1. I'm in the shower,

2. At night when everyone is asleep, or

3. When I'm alone in a store.

I'll say to myself, "Gee, you should really talk to the kids about that. They would be interested in that. It would make them better to know that".

Then, when those very same children are all around me, all I can think about is what they're saying to me, or what we're physically doing. All of those interesting things I had lined up to talk to them about take a backseat to the *I want a snack*'s and *I'm bleeding*'s and *Are you **sure** Sharpies are permanent?*

So, I started to make myself some notes. I collected enough yellow sticky post-its on one topic to clump them into a theme. Then I made more notes on more themes, and before I knew it, I had a year's worth of weekly themes and several yellow stickies for each.

But the themes and notes weren't enough, because I couldn't remember what the one-word notes meant. *Yes, I had something to say about that, but what exactly was it, again?*

"Hey guys, about Thanksgiving. I'd love to talk to you about – um, turkey, and – big boats. And buckle shoes."

I'll admit it- I dumped most of the information I learned in third grade to make room for what I learned in fourth grade. Then I dumped fourth grade to make room for fifth grade, and so on and so forth. Any facts I had picked up in school are now so much more than hazy.

I realized I needed actual words to put into my own mouth if I was going to speak intelligently about the topics I'd hoped would be interesting to these dear offspring of mine. And forget it if anything, and I mean *anything* else was going on around us; It was just not physically possible for me to think about American history as I tied someone's shoe.

So, after a spate of fact-checking and topic-testing on my own, sweet, little guinea-pigs (and any other child physically near enough to get roped into our frequent schemes), I do believe we ended up with an arguably educational resource that we can put to good use with our families.

Or at least look enthusiastic carrying around.

For Which Kids?

The information in this book is ideally targeted to 3 to 8 year-old kids, but you can simplify the concepts for littler ones or make them more challenging for older ones.

For Younger Kids (Under 3):

You could also:

- Show them pictures of what you're talking about.
- Draw them pictures of what you're talking about.
- Instead of following the notes exactly for each day of the week, pick the two easiest days and do them twice, each.
- Talk to them at times other than the witching hour.
- Use your hands to act out what you're talking about.

For the Big Guys (Over 8):

You could also:

- Quiz them on what you taught them at a later time during the day.
- Omit key pieces of information and see if they can guess what's missing.
- Have them finish your sentences.
- Have them tell you what they already know about the topic, and you fill in any gaps.
- Have them give report outs to Mom, Dad or siblings.

Free Weeks:

Because I wanted us to be able to use these lessons during any calendar year (and over and over again if we so desire), I had to take one notable liberty:

To make sure we are giving lessons close to when the actual holidays and special events occur each year, I wrote four weeks of lesson plans for each calendar month. 4 weeks X 12 months = 48 weekly themes. But, since there are 52 weeks in the year, (and 52 weeks – 48 weeks = 4), we'll have a total of four free weeks each year to fill in with whatever the heck we want to, like:

★ Reviewing our favorite lessons
★ Taking library trips
★ Going to the zoo
★ Going to the museum
★ Going to the spa (hey - being the boss has its perks).

Best Time to Give a Lesson Plan:

When should you give these little lesson plans to your own kids? Well, it's really entirely up to you. Sure, you could sit your darlings down at the table and give them a wholesome, scholarly recitation each weekday that favors a scene out of the countryside schoolhouse on *Little House on the Prairie.*

I should be so lucky.

The rest of us might fare better by keeping this book in the kitchen or the car. I know in our house everyone seems to pay attention to me when I am holding their food (or extra-curricular activities) hostage.

It might take a couple of practice lessons to figure out the optimal time to present this information to your own child. You certainly don't need to stick with breakfast or carpool. If you have another break in your day when you are sitting down together (and you don't mind committing ten minutes of that togetherness to a lesson); go for it.

But, a friendly note of warning: The less distracted your child is, the better. If the TV or Wii is on in the background, you're toast.

Also, I hate to point out the obvious, but don't forget to consider whether your child is a morning person or a night person. *You* know. Oh, Sister/Brother do you know this information all-too well.

Good to Know:

Another friendly something to keep in mind: You may notice your child guides you enthusiastically through some of the lessons (if he likes or is already familiar with the topic), while other times he may seem to be tuning you out altogether. Don't worry. The important thing is that you're having the conversation, which opens the door for him to think and talk about new things.

Maybe he has nothing to say about it at first, but don't be surprised if he whips out some random fact you taught him three weeks later, with a very matter-of-fact delivery. You'll say, "Now, where did you learn that?", and he'll say, "I can't remember", but that's okay. You can still feel really good about it, because you and I both know it was *you* who taught it to him.

Also, let's just get this out there: I'm gonna call your child "he" through all of the lessons. If I don't, you're going to get forward-slashed to death with all of the he / shes and him / hers.

And lastly, a large monkey clip and inexpensive cookbook stand sufficiently put the lessons up in our daily business. This helps those of us whom tend to distract easily (me included).

(Better odds you'll use the book)

Oh! The Founding Fathers Were THOSE Guys!

Also, please don't get sweaty and embarrassed if any of the information in these lesson plans is new to you, too. I learned much more than I care to admit in doing "research for the children".

Once you read through the lessons (and make that knowledge your own), you have a very difficult decision:

Do you act like you always knew these things, or do you confess your elementary school shortcomings?

I personally do a little of both. Hey- even Oprah had a teleprompter!

It's time to fill those sippy cups to capacity. Your child's year of little lessons begins now.

Courtney Loquasto

January Week 1: The Calendar

✳ *Monday* - Chat about what we use the calendar for, including:

- ★ Tracking which day of the week, month and year it is
- ★ Marking special occasions
- ★ Finding out when holidays are, and
- ★ Gauging how long we have until special milestones, like your birthday.

Show your child examples of different calendars you have in the house (electronic planner, big desk calendar, wall calendar, free junk mail wallet calendar).

Explain that each calendar day is based on one rotation of the earth, or 24 hours, or one day + one night.

Interesting facts: Here is how one year breaks down, in different time units:

- ★ 12 months
- ★ 52 weeks
- ★ 365 days

★ *8,760 hours*

★ *525,600 minutes*

★ *31,536,000 seconds.*

It's funny to deliver this to the kids like you're computing the numbers in your head. "Let's see – 365 days is…carry the 2…8,760" and so on.

✳ *Tuesday* - Go over the names of the different days of the week. For little-little guys, repeat the days of the week a few times to get them familiar with how they sound in order. For bigger kids, ask them tricky questions about the week, like: "What is 3 days after Monday?" (Thursday), or: "What is today, minus 2 days, plus 5 days, minus 3 days?" (Today).

✳ *Wednesday* - Introduce (or revisit) the four seasons- Winter, Spring, Summer, Fall. Tell your child which season is your favorite (and why), and ask him which is his favorite and why.

✳ *Thursday* - Talk about the biggie holidays and the months that they generally fall into. Quiz bigger kids to see if they can remember which holidays are when:

★ January: MLK Day

★ February: Valentine's Day

★ March: St. Patrick's Day

★ March/ April: Easter

★ May: Memorial Day

★ July: Independence Day

★ September: Labor Day

★ October: Halloween

★ November: Thanksgiving

★ November/ December: Hanukkah

★ December: Christmas, New Year's Eve

Assign each child an extended family member and have him interview him / her to find out their favorite holiday and why.

❊ Friday - With your child, enter the birthdays of your family members into a calendar, including grandparents, aunts, uncles, and cousins. Once you have entered them all in, go month-by-month and notice together the months that contain a lot of your family's birthdays, as well as those that don't have any.

Courtney Loquasto

January Week 2: Family Tree

✴ *Monday* - Explain that a family tree is a chart that describes the relationships between different members in a family, and it can take on the general shape of a tree. There are lots of different versions of a family tree, but here is a simple example:

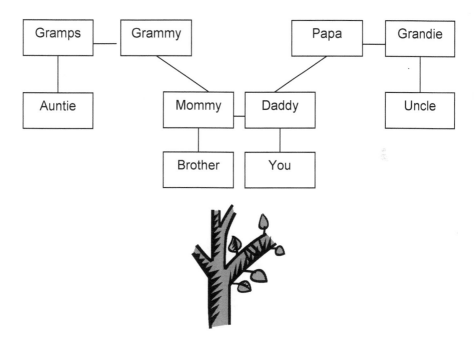

✴ *Tuesday* - Together with your child, get out a good size sheet of paper and a pencil with an eraser. Start at the bottom of the tree, [which would be your own kid(s)], and work your way up your own family tree as best you can.

If you can't remember the names of your great-grandparents, have your child help you with your research, and write a letter together to your parents or other living family members asking for information. Writing letters and getting mail is wildly exciting for the 8-year-old and under set!

✳ *Wednesday* - Pretty up your tree with paint, construction paper, glitter, sequins; the whole nine. Make sure you leave blank space where you can fill in the missing relatives you're waiting to hear back about.

✳ *Thursday* - Talk about why it's important (and interesting) to know your extended family. Different reasons you could give include:

- You get a good feeling knowing you are closely connected to a lot of different people
- You may be very interested in what your ancestors did
- This is your "team"
- You might be related to somebody famous in history
- You might look just like your great-great grandma or grandpa.

✳ *Friday* - A quote for your week, by Bishop Desmond Tutu (a South African spiritual leader and activist, born in 1931):

You don't choose your family. They are God's gift to you, as you are to them.

Courtney Loquasto

January Week 3: Winter Sports

✳ *Monday* - Talk about all of the different sports you can play in the winter. Some of them include basketball, hockey, ice skating, skiing and snowboarding. If you've ever done any of these, tell your child about your experience. If your child has done any of them, have him share his favorite stories.

✳ *Tuesday* - Explain that basketball is a sport where you only need one person to practice shooting hoops, dribbling and running down the court, and two people for a game (though to play an organized basketball game, you would need 5 players on each team, for a total of 10 players). Each team tries to score the most points by shooting the ball in the hoop.

If you have a little-little guy, you can take a squishy ball and show him how to drop it into a laundry basket, and then let him try it. For a bigger kid, you can have him aim that same squishy ball at an empty laundry hamper a good distance away that is pushed against a wall.

Interesting fact: The tallest person to play point guard in the NBA was Magic Johnson, at 6 feet 9 inches.

✳ **Wednesday**- Introduce (or revisit) the game of ice hockey. Two teams try to score against each other by knocking a rubber puck into the opponent's goal. The game is played on an ice rink and all of the players wear hockey skates. There are 6 players on each team: 5 "skaters" and 1 goaltender.

The players wear a lot of protective gear. Here is a list of some of the things a goaltender wears. (You could make reading this list into a little game by having your child point to where on his body he thinks each goes):

★ Goalie mask
★ Chest/ arm protectors
★ Blocking glove
★ Goalie glove
★ Goal jock (boys) or pelvic protector (girls)
★ Goal pants
★ Thigh guards
★ Knee pads
★ Toe caps

★ Wrist guards

★ Goal pads (for legs, shin, knees)

★ Knee socks (for calf protection)

★ Helmet

★ Neck protector

★ Hockey throat guard.

✳ **Thursday**- Introduce (or revisit) ice skating. The three main types are recreational ice skating, figure skating, and speed skating.

Recreational ice skating can be done at a commercial ice rink, a lake/ pond that is very, very frozen, or even in a homemade back yard ice rink. Some tips for beginning ice skaters:

@ Try walking in your skates (with the skate guards on) on solid ground before trying them on ice.

@ To catch your balance, hold your arms out just below your shoulders, bend your knees slightly, and lean forward a little.

@ If you feel like you're about to fall, bend your knees and squat into the ice, breaking the fall with your hands. Be careful of other skaters zooming by!

@ To get up, get on your hands and knees and put one foot between your hands. When you're steady, bring the other foot between your hands, keep your feet slightly apart, and slowly stand up.

@ Especially for kids, a helmet wouldn't hurt here!

Figure skating describes a sport where people perform spins, jumps and other dance-like moves on ice. There are all different levels of figure skating competitions, from beginner to Olympic.

Interesting fact: According to the International Skating Union, ladies must wear skirts and men must wear full-length trousers; no tights.

Speed skating describes competitive racing on speed skates, usually around an oval course. There are two different types of speed skating events in the winter Olympics, long track speed skating and short track speed skating. The current world record for the 1500 meter was set by the American Shani Davis on March 7, 2009. He was clocked skating 33.68 miles per hour. Point out how fast that is the next time you're in the car.

✳ *Friday* - Introduce (or revisit) skiing (which includes snowboarding).

The term *skiing* includes lots of variations of people traveling on skis, or, long runners made of plastic, wood or metal that attach to ski boots. In the Winter Olympics, there are 6 different skiing events:

1. Alpine (downhill)
2. Cross Country (countryside)
3. Freestyle (acrobatic downhill skiing)
4. Nordic Combined (cross country and ski jumping)
5. Ski Jumping (skiing off a ramp)
6. Snowboarding (one wide ski that attaches to both feet)

In snowboarder lingo, you skate "goofy" if you snowboard with your right foot in front.

Courtney Loquasto

January Week 4: Recycling

✴ *Monday* - Talk about why recycling is good in kid-terms, including:

- ❧ We don't want to waste anything if someone can use it again.
- ❧ It takes the junk out of the trash that doesn't break down into nature on it's own (and, if we use less space for garbage, we have more space for pretty things).
- ❧ We don't have to go out and spend our money on new things if we can use what we have (and, in turn, save our money for other uses).
- ❧ We can save natural resources (trees, water, minerals) for the future, instead of using them up now.
- ❧ We can prevent some of the pollution companies create when they make new products from scratch.

✴ *Tuesday* - Explore the ideas of **Reduce** (use only what you need), **Reuse** (think about creative uses for items, besides what they were originally used for), and **Recycle** (put certain things aside for recycling so they can be used again).

- @ **Reduce**- Do a little experiment with your child. Sprinkle a little water on the counter. See how much of a paper towel it takes to soak it up. Maybe half? A quarter? The rest was wasted. Make the point that we only want to use what we need in this type of situation.

- @ **Reuse**- Take a plain ol' box and plop it on the table. See how many creative uses your kid(s) can come up with for other uses for the box other than trash.

- @ **Recycle**- Go over common things we can recycle, like batteries, cans, paper, plastic, glass, magazines, newspapers, paint, oil, appliances, tires, electronics, and yard waste.

☀ *Wednesday*- Get your family's recycling plan in order. Go around the house with your child and gather up and consolidate everything you can recycle.

Do you have a service that comes to your house to pick up recyclables? Great, you're all set! Do you have to drive your recyclables to a local center? A little more of an effort, but you'll feel better once it's out of your house and your conscious is clean, right? (Earth911.com is a good site to find recycling locations near where you live.)

If you are required to separate your recyclables, consider putting aside some larger plastic containers with a label for what goes in there (glass, plastic, paper). Those little ones learn so quickly what can be recycled and where they belong that you may find you have more help on an ongoing basis than you originally expected.

❋ Thursday – Interesting recycling fact: According to the Environmental Protection Agency, in 2008 an average American produced about 4.5 pounds of waste each day.

How much does your child weigh? How many days would it take to produce enough trash to balance on the other side of a see-saw from him?

❋ Friday – Jack Johnson has a song, "3 Rs" (Reduce, Reuse, Recycle) from the *Sing-a-Longs and Lullabies for the Film Curious George* CD. It fits nicely with this week's theme, so you may want to consider downloading it or reserving the CD at the library.

Courtney Loquasto

February Week 1: Teeth

✳ *Monday*- Review proper dental care, including brushing at least twice a day, flossing once a day, and checkups twice a year. Give a flossing lesson with a flashlight and flossing sticks (which can be found at almost any general store).

✳ *Tuesday*- Talk about what happens when you lose a tooth. Don't forget the wonderful, gory details, like:

★ First you notice you can wiggle your tooth a little bit with your finger
★ Then you can wiggle it a lot with your finger
★ Then you can wiggle it with your tongue
★ Then you can stick your tongue inside the hole between your tooth and your gum
★ Then it's hanging just by a thread
★ Then (usually painlessly) it comes out when it's ready
★ It's about the size of a pea
★ Then you clean it off and put it under your pillow

★ Then the tooth fairy comes and leaves you a little money in exchange for the tooth!

*Note to first time Tooth Fairies: You may want to do a little research locally about what the going rate for a first tooth is. Kids talk, especially about this.

✵ Wednesday - Describe a typical trip to the dentist. If he's been already, have him talk about what he remembers. Talk about the different things you go through at a typical visit, like:

- "When you go to the dentist, you check in at the front desk and sit in the waiting room. Someone comes out and calls your name, usually a dental hygienist, and she or he takes you to the chair that you will sit in for your visit.

- Once you are in your chair, the dental hygienist cleans your teeth, either with a regular toothbrush or a spin brush. She or he then rinses your mouth out with water from a neat little contraption that looks like a mini-watering can, and you can either spit it out, or they can put a mini-vacuum in your mouth to suck up the water. Then she or he flosses your teeth. You may or may not get pictures taken of your teeth, which is very easy; you just bite down on a piece of plastic and they snap a shot.

@ The dentist then looks at your teeth and makes sure you don't have any cavities. If you do have a cavity, the dentist very gently fills it so it isn't a cavity anymore. Sometimes you get a balloon or a toy when you leave."

✳ **Thursday**- **Interesting fact**: George Washington had dentures made of hippopotamus ivory and gold.

✳ **Friday**- Let everyone who is due pick out a new toothbrush at the store.

Courtney Loquasto

February Week 2: Love

☀ *Monday*- Talk to your child about how you unconditionally love him (meaning you love him regardless of what he might do or say). You can explain that within our families, we may get mad at each other, but that doesn't change the love we have for each other.

And conversely, winning awards or being good (though it makes us very proud) doesn't make us love each other any more than we already do.

> ℮ Kids don't inherently know this, so it can't hurt to reiterate it once in awhile, and what better month to do so? You could also mention that God always loves us, too; no matter what.

☀ *Tuesday*- Explain (or review) the idea that Valentine's Day is a day we set aside to tell our friends, family, husband/significant others, wives, boyfriends and girlfriends how we feel about them. That is why we exchange valentines with each other; to remind one another that they are special to us.

@ The first valentine cards were exchanged in America in the early 1700s. In 1850, a woman named Ester Howland, nicknamed the "Mother of the American Valentine", ran an ad in a Massachusetts newspaper to sell pretty, ornate valentines that were made to look like an English valentine she had received.

@ She ran an assembly-line in her house to fulfill the valentine orders that came in. The valentines became very popular, and her business thrived. Those early valentines had ribbons, lace, and colorful pictures called *scrap* on them.

✳ **Wednesday** Talk about some famous couples throughout history –

★ Adam and Eve (Biblical)
★ Antony and Cleopatra (infamous love affair between Caesar's cousin and the queen of Egypt, circa 40 BC),
★ Romeo and Juliet (fictitious characters in a Shakespearian Tragedy)
★ Bonnie and Clyde (real-life infamous partners-in-crime in the 1930's).

✳ **Thursday** Introduce Cupid, the god of love in Roman Mythology, who is depicted as a cherubic angel boy with wings and a bow and arrow. Tell your child that anyone hit by one of his arrows falls in love with the next person they see, so be careful...

✳ *Friday*- Get out some construction paper and the prettiest decorative things you can find, including glitter, stickers, lace doilies, magazine pictures of people in love, sequins, feathers, pretty buttons, pom-poms and/ or some pretty colored markers or crayons.

You and he take ten minutes to make a few valentines for your nearest and dearest. (Your significant other would probably love one from you, too, don't forget. You know how he/she loves your art projects.)

Courtney Loquasto

February Week 3: Black History

※ *Monday* – Talk about the Reverend Martin Luther King Jr, who was a Nobel Peace Prize winning champion of equal rights for African-Americans. This might be somewhat of a familiar topic for your family, since MLK day was in January.

- The plight MLK Jr. faced may be difficult for children to understand, especially if they are (hopefully) not yet aware of prejudice or racism in their young lives. MLK was assassinated by gunshot in 1968, and this is also a very heavy topic for very young kids.

- You could explain, though, that the Reverend was a great man who fought very hard to convince people to be nice to each other and to treat each other as equals, and he did so in a peaceful way. A lot of people listened to him, and many, many people's lives are better because of the work he did in the 1950's and 1960's.

  You could also tell your kids that MLK gave a very famous 17-minute speech called "I Have a Dream" from the steps of the Lincoln Memorial in Washington, D.C. in 1963.

Over 200,000 people gathered on the National Mall (which is the long, open space that runs from the US Capitol Building to the Washington Monument) to hear his speech.

MLK talked about his hope that our country would follow the groundwork that our Founding Fathers laid out for us, and that it would become a nation where everyone was treated as equals.

✳ *Tuesday*- Discuss the fact that President Barack Obama, the 44th President of the United States, was the first African-American US president ever elected.

His father was from Kenya and his mother was from Kansas. Once he went to law school, he became the first African-American president of the Harvard Law Review. Before becoming president, he served both as an Illinois State Senator and a United States Senator.

President Obama's wife's name is Michelle, and they have two daughters, Malia and Sasha. Their dog's name is Bo.

✳ *Wednesday*- Talk about General Colin Powell, the first African-American to become the Chairman of Joint Chiefs of Staff as well as US Secretary of State (or, for little guys, "some really big US government jobs").

He was born in Harlem, NY in 1937 and was the son of Jamaican immigrants who worked in the garment district.

Also:

- He:
  - ★ Served in the Vietnam War
  - ★ Was awarded 2 Purple Hearts,
  - ★ A Bronze Star,
  - ★ A Soldier's medal, and
  - ★ The Legion of Merit (or, "big-time military awards").

- President George H.W. Bush named him to be the Chairman of the Joint Chiefs of Staff (or, the "top boss of the military" and "the person who gives military advice to the President").

- After that, some people even talked about General Powell running for President or Vice President of the US, but he didn't want to do that.

  He didn't like the idea of himself or his family being in the spotlight like that. He did, however, say yes to serving with another President Bush years later: President George W. Bush, as his Secretary of State (or, "the person who gives advice to the President about policies with other countries").

✹ *Thursday*- Talk about Oprah Winfrey. Explain that she is an African-American TV show host, actress, producer and philanthropist (or, "TV star, movie star, lady who helps create shows and person who does really good things for other people").

@ Oprah had a rough childhood growing up. She got into radio and television broadcasting when she was older, and then hosted talk shows in Baltimore and Chicago.

@ She launched her own show, **"The Oprah Winfrey Show"**, in 1986. It was really popular, and she regularly gave nice things to the people who came to watch her show. Sometimes she even gave them cars.

@ Oprah has helped (and continues to help) a lot of people. She:

- Started a leadership academy for girls in South Africa, and

- Created (and paid for the expenses associated with) the Oprah's Angel Network, which is a charity that raised more than $80,000,000 for charitable projects and grants around the world.

That number is a little less than how many miles the earth is from the sun (93,000,000 miles).

✳ *Friday* - Review who you talked about this week.

See what your child remembers on his own about each person you discussed.

Courtney Loquasto

February Week 4: U.S. Presidents

✳ *Monday* - Introduce (or revisit) the first president of the United States, George Washington.

Explain (as best you can to little guys) that he was elected unanimously (nobody voted against him) by the Electoral College, which was made up of the representatives elected by each state to choose our president. He was elected in 1789.

- There was a story about George when he was a young boy and a cherry tree. The story has been told over and over again, though it has never been scientifically proven to have actually occurred. Nonetheless, the story goes that George cut down his father's cherry tree. When asked if he did it, George replied, "I cannot tell a lie".

- Go ahead and milk this story, whether it's true or not, and talk about how people with great character do not lie, and that it is always better to tell the truth. George grew up to be a great man, and many historians consider him to be one of the top two or three presidents of all time.

@ See if anyone can guess which type of money has George Washington's face on it? (The dollar).

✳ *Tuesday*- Explain that we celebrate President's Day on the third Monday in February, to recognize the birthdays of George Washington (Feb 22, 1732) and Abraham Lincoln (February 12, 1809).

✳ *Wednesday*- **Interesting fact**: The shortest US president was James Madison (1809-1817), at 5'4". Our tallest two presidents were Abraham Lincoln (1861-1865) and Lyndon B. Johnson (1963-1969), both 6'4".

@ Point out people you know that are 5'4" and 6'4" to give your child some perspective on how short/ tall these measurements are.

✳ *Thursday*- Talk about the different US presidents throughout history who were related. Twice we elected a father and son president:

@ John Adams (1797-1801) and John Quincy Adams (1825-1829), and
@ George H. Bush (1989-1993) and George W. Bush (2001-2009).

Once we elected a grandfather and grandson president; William Henry Harrison (1841) and Benjamin Harrison (1889-1893).

Theodore Roosevelt (1901-1909) and Franklin D. Roosevelt (1933-1945) were 5th cousins, but they were even more closely related because Franklin married Theodore's niece (Eleanor).

Are you related to anyone that has the job that your child says he wants to do when he grows up? For example, was your father a police officer (and your son wants to be one, too?)

✳ *Friday* **Another interesting fact:** Many of our presidents were lawyers, soldiers or government officials before they became president. However, many former presidents had jobs that had nothing to do with the military or government before they took office. Here are a few examples:

★ Andrew Johnson (1865-1869) was a tailor

★ Warren G. Harding (1921-1923) was a newspaper editor

★ Jimmy Carter (1977-1981) was a peanut farmer

★ Ronald Reagan (1981-1989) was a movie star.

Courtney Loquasto

March Week 1: Spring Cleaning

✳ *Monday* - Explain that spring cleaning is an organized, thorough cleaning of our homes that many people do at the end of winter.

The reason we do this when the weather starts to get warmer is because we feel like we've been cooped up all winter and are ready to get out. Now we can open the windows and shake the dust and dirt that's been collecting while we were stuck inside our homes.

Have your child declare what area of his is the messiest or dirtiest. Closets, bathtubs, bedroom windows, under beds, chests of drawers and book bags are all fair game.

If you have more than one child, give an award to the person whom you deem the owner of the most unkempt situation. He doesn't even know what's coming…

✳ *Tuesday* - Teach (or re-teach) your child the basic cleaning moves (sweeping, dusting, vacuuming, cleaning windows, picking up toys, etc.), as appropriate for his age.

Have him help organize sock drawers and closets.

Put on your "Fun Parent" face and show him how to fold towels and sheets as a 2-person team ("You hold two corners, I'll hold two corners, and let's meet in the middle. Now I hold two corners, you grab the two new corners at the bottom, and let's meet in the middle", and so on).

✳ *Wednesday* - Work together to start the process of switching out clothes for the warmer season.

Don't worry if it's still cold outside. This process could take you a couple of months if you include your child.

Maybe longer.

Some things you could get him started on now include:

> ❷ Have him separate his clothes into cold and warm-weather piles, then have him help you find a place to keep each until it's time to get rid of the cold weather items.

- @ Have him help you launder all the cold-season clothes, fold them and repair them when necessary.

- @ Have him help you decide what you are going to do with the clothes once you are done with them. Do they get donated? Do they go to a younger sibling? Are you going to sell them on eBay?

It's a pain switching out all of those clothes, but you'll feel so much better once it's done, right?

Well, that and you won't have to feel guilty about being the one who sent his/ her kid to the pool party in a turtleneck.

* **Thursday**- Pick a more complicated cleaning project to attack as a family. Set aside ten minutes today to write out your plan for who is responsible for what, in what time frame, and what the payoff will be.

The prize could be as simple as the satisfaction of having that space clean and livable for your family. Or, you could go the unabashed bribery route, and dangle a trip to the ice cream shop out there like a carrot.

Some ideas for the family cleaning project:

★ Clean and organize the garage

★ Clean out the attic

★ Clean out the basement

★ Clean the patio/ deck/ porch

★ Clean and organize the play area/ room.

✳ *Friday*- Work on the project you picked yesterday, and then walk around as a family to admire all of the good work you put in this week.

(This is a good weekend to have your in-laws visit, by the way.)

March Week 2: Birthdays

✳ *Monday*- Have you ever heard of a **Golden Birthday**? It's the year a person turns the age of their birth date. So, for example, if you are born on March 14th, your Golden Birthday is your 14th birthday.

Figure out each family member's Golden Birthday, and whether it's anytime soon, a long ways off, or missed completely.

For those who missed a Golden Birthday: Draw a golden cupcake and cut it out for that person. Sing "Happy Golden Birthday to You" and let them blow out the pretend candles.

✳ *Tuesday*- Do a quick Google search (together) of each family member's birth date. Talk about famous events and famous birthdays you discover for each of your dates.

✳ *Wednesday*- Explain to your child that there is a special birthstone assigned to each month. Their birthstone is the one for the month in which they were born.

See if your child already knows what his birthstone is. If not (or if you are foggy yourself), here is a review of birthstones by month:

- ★ Jan. - Garnet (deep, rich red)
- ★ Feb. - Amethyst (purple or violet)
- ★ Mar. - Aquamarine (pale blue-green)
- ★ Apr. - Diamond (clear)
- ★ May - Emerald (green)
- ★ June - Pearl (opaque white or ivory)
- ★ July - Ruby (red)
- ★ Aug. - Peridot (pale yellow-green)
- ★ Sep. - Sapphire (deep, navy blue)
- ★ Oct. - Opal (multi-color, pink)
- ★ Nov. - Topaz (yellow)
- ★ Dec. — Turquoise (blue)

✹ Thursday- Share funny or interesting family birthday stories. For example, in the 80's, many of my family members loved the movie **Strange Brew**. In it, the stars (who played Canadian ne'er-do-wells) called each other "Hosers". So, to be funny, my mom ordered my 10th birthday cake with the words *Happy Birthday Courtney, You Hoser* to be written on it.

But there was a misunderstanding at the cake shop. When my mother opened the cake box in front of all of my little girlfriends, it said *Happy Birthday Courtney, You Loser.*

If it's early and you can't come up with a story on your own, you are more than welcome to use that one.

✳ *Friday* - Quote for the week, by Lewis Carroll, from *Through the Looking Glass:*

There are three hundred and sixty-four days when you might get un-birthday presents, and only one for birthday presents, you know.

Courtney Loquasto

March Week 3: The Color Green

✳ *Monday*- Explain that by mixing the primary colors yellow and blue, you can make green.

Show how this works with poster paint or watercolor paint. Demonstrate what happens if you use more yellow than blue (you should get a yellow-green), and then what happens if you use more blue than yellow (you should get a blue-green).

Now, if you dare (and no one is getting their picture taken that day) let him try it out.

Or, you could just point out what happens to the blue and yellow lines as you zip his sandwich bag shut.

✳ *Tuesday*- Take turns with your child naming everything you can think of that's green. See how long you can go.

Since you are the parent (and we are here to look out for each other), here are some cheats for you in case you run out of answers. It's very good for you if your child thinks you are all-knowing, for as long as humanly possible.

Green things (in no order):

- ★ Lettuce
- ★ Celery
- ★ Avocados
- ★ Grass
- ★ Broccoli
- ★ Cucumbers
- ★ Leprechauns
- ★ Iguanas
- ★ Apples
- ★ Paper Money
- ★ Pickles
- ★ Green Peppers
- ★ Lily Pads
- ★ Leaves
- ★ Green Beans
- ★ Moss
- ★ Grasshoppers
- ★ Christmas Trees
- ★ Peas
- ★ Olives
- ★ Limes
- ★ Zucchinis
- ★ Kermit the Frog

✳ **Wednesday**- The world around you is about to turn green again! Point out tiny buds on the trees and the sprouts from the first spring flowers as you see them throughout your day.

✳ **Thursday**- **Interesting Fact**: Why do we wear green on St. Patrick's Day? For the green in Ireland's flag, Ireland's nickname, *The Emerald Isle,* and in reference to its lush, green landscape.

Don't forget to dress your child in green on March 17th. Explain that if he doesn't have green on, he could get pinched. There's always that *one* kid in the class who's on a mission with the pinching!

[Quick review for you so you can properly introduce the country of Ireland: The geography is a tiny bit confusing because Ireland (the sovereign country) takes up most of the island also called *Ireland*, but the northern one-sixth of the island is called *Northern Ireland*, and belongs to the United Kingdom. The Republic of Ireland (or *Eire)* has about 4.5 million people. Dublin is its largest city. This may be TMI for your kid(s), but good to have in your back pocket in case it comes up.]

✳ *Friday* - St. Patty's Day Joke:

Why can't you borrow money from a leprechaun?

Because they're always a little short!

March Week 4: Temperature

☀ *Monday* - Explain that there are 3 scales used to measure temperature:

1. *Fahrenheit* (freezing is 32°F, boiling is 212°F)

2. *Celsius* (freezing is 0°C, boiling is 100°C)

3. *Kelvin* (the same increments as the Celsius scale, but begins at absolute zero, which is -273.15°C or -459.67°F)

Only the United States, Belize and Jamaica use Fahrenheit for domestic use.

☀ *Tuesday* - **Interesting fact**: The hottest temperature ever recorded in the world was 136° F (57.8 ° C), in Al 'Aziziya, Libya on September 12, 1922.

You can cook an egg at 158 ° F.

The coldest temperature ever recorded in the world was -128.6° F (-89.2° C) at Volskok Station, Antarctica on July 21, 1983.

✳ **Wednesday** - Introduce (or revisit) the thermometer.

Thermometers are able to measure temperature because they contain materials that change in some way when they are heated or cooled.

Galileo invented a water thermometer in 1593, and then Gabriel Fahrenheit invented the first modern mercury thermometer in 1714. In 1724 he invented the Fahrenheit temperature scale.

Many of us are used to holding a thermometer under our tongue or arm to take our temperature, but other common thermometers measure the temperature in our ear and on our forehead.

✳ **Thursday** - An easy, interesting temperature experiment to do in the morning and check in the afternoon:

Morning: Pour a cup of water into a clear plastic container (like a clear plastic cup). Add a couple of tablespoons of cooking oil, and let is sit for a couple of minutes. Where does the oil go? Jot down your answer and put the mixture into the freezer and let it sit for a few hours.

Afternoon: Check on your concoction.

Now where is the oil?

✳ *Friday* – Just for fun, if you have an oral thermometer, take your child's temperature. Then have him chew on some crushed ice or drink cold water, and take his temperature again. Point out how quickly his temperature changed.

Courtney Loquasto

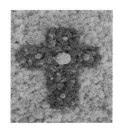

April Week 1: Easter

✳ *Monday*- Talk about any family Easter traditions you have.

- ★ Do you hunt for eggs?
- ★ Does the Easter Bunny deliver baskets to your house?
- ★ Do you go to church and then have a big meal as a family?
- ★ Are there any new ones you'd like to try this year?

In my home, there is always a good bit of indecision about what to serve for Easter dinner, since we're not a big ham-lovin' family.

If your family has the same ham-aversion issue, you could consider pairing a leg or rack of lamb with mint sauce and some of these traditional accompaniments:

- ★ Asparagus (roasted, steamed, dressed or plain)

★ Hot-cross buns (lightly sweetened cinnamon yeast buns)

★ Sugar snap peas

★ Baked macaroni and cheese.

@ And remember, the more input you allow your child in the planning of this special meal, the more leverage you have when you ask him to help you cook it.

And eat it.

And clean up after it!

✳ Tuesday - Why do we decorate Easter eggs?

Interesting fact: According to the Catholic Encyclopedia, eating eggs was forbidden during Lent. Once Lent was over, eggs were dyed red to celebrate Easter joy, and everyone who avoided them during Lent ate them. Thus, Easter became a big egg day.

✳ Wednesday - How to dye Easter eggs with natural dyes:

For each color, use a separate pot (or make one color at a time in the same pot). Follow these directions completely for each color:

★ Bring 1 qt. water, 2 tbs vinegar, and the colored item (from list below) to a boil. Use more of the colored item for a stronger color, less for a paler color.

★ Simmer 30 minutes.

★ Strain liquid into bowl and cool.

★ Soak hard boiled egg in colored liquid for as short as 5 minutes, as long as overnight (in fridge).

★ Remove egg, let dry, and store in fridge.

Natural Dyes:

1. Blue: Canned blueberries

2. Yellow: Turmeric

3. Red: Crushed raspberries

✳ Thursday- Here's a suggestion on how to explain the concept of (Christian) Easter in terms your very young child can understand and hopefully not get nightmares about:

"This is the time of year when we celebrate Jesus going to Heaven. God had Jesus go to Heaven so that the rest of us could, too, when He calls us."

A note of warning, though - If you have not yet introduced Heaven or dying in any way, this might bring that conversation up. If you're not ready for that, you may want to stick to talking about how important it is to think about Jesus often, but especially during this time of year.

✳ *Friday* - Easter is a time of celebration after a somber, reflective period.

This is a very legitimate reason to hork down several pieces of good Easter chocolate.

April Week 2: Rain

✳ *Monday*- April showers bring May flowers.

Say it, explain it, let it sink in. Take questions.

If you have a little one that is afraid of lightning and thunder, here are some ideas to take the edge off:

- Don't show any anxiety or fear during thunderstorms yourself.
- Tell him to think of thunder as God teaching the angels to bowl or play the drums.
- Remind him that rainstorms are a good thing. They water all of the grass, trees, flowers and bushes around us.
- If it's daytime, point out that there might be a rainbow at the end of the storm and look for one together when it stops raining.
- Have him make his own thunder by blowing up a paper lunch bag, twisting the opening shut, and then popping the bag to make a good-sized boom. It might help him to feel like he is in control of the noise, and he might even want to do it

over and over again once he realizes it's not so bad.

✳ *Tuesday* **Interesting fact**: Rain boots are also called galoshes, mudders and wellies. The next time it rains, see who can make the highest splash, as well as the farthest-reaching splash.

Give valuable pretend prizes.

✳ *Wednesday* **Another interesting fact**: The word *umbrella* comes from the Latin word "umbra", which means shade or shadow.

Lots of kids love umbrellas. Does everyone who's old enough to handle it have their own, working umbrella in your house? Ones with broken spindles or the tendency to flip inside-out in a light wind, though wildly exciting to the younger set, don't technically count as "working".

If you're willing to spare a little extra cash the next time you're at the store, let each person pick out their own new umbrella. You could even use it as a good behavior motivator for a couple of days preceding your purchase.

You might actually be very happy you did this the next time your family has to make a run for it during a downpour.

✳ *Thursday*- April joke:

How many animals did Moses take on the arch?

None; It was Noah!

✳ *Friday*- Have your child make his own rain gauge.

1. Put a cup outside the next time it rains, and then

2. Measure how much water accumulated in it with a ruler.

3. Watch the cup over the next couple of days and

4. Point out how long it takes for the water to completely evaporate.

Courtney Loquasto

April Week 3: Baseball / Softball

✳ *Monday*- Explain that in high school and college, softball teams consist primarily of girls, while baseball teams consist mostly of boys. Young children and adult baseball and softball teams tend to be more a mix of males and females.

✳ *Tuesday*- Teach the lyrics to the song "Take Me Out to the Ballgame" (by Jack Norworth, 1928) to your child. He (and you) may need to use it this summer!

In case you need a refresher, here are the words:

> Take me out to the ballgame,
>
> Take me out with the crowd.
>
> Buy me some peanuts and Cracker Jack,
>
> I don't care if I never get back,
>
> Let me root, root, root for the home team,
>
> If they don't win it's a shame.

For its one, two, three strikes you're out

At the old ball game!

✳ **Wednesday** - Run through some facts about Babe Ruth, known by many as the greatest baseball player of all time.

Here are a few:

- He was born in 1895 as George Herman Ruth, in Baltimore, MD.
- Some of his nicknames include: The Babe, The Bambino, and The Sultan of Swat.
- He set many records while playing for the Boston Red Sox and NY Yankees.
- Yankee Stadium, built in 1923, was dubbed *The House that Ruth Built.*

✳ **Thursday** - Break down some popular pitches:

- **Curveball**: A type of pitch that curves either towards or away from the batter.
- **Fastball**: A pitch thrown at a very high speed with little curve. Also the most common type of pitch in baseball.
- **Changeup**: A pitch thrown with relatively little velocity, when the batter is expecting a fastball.

✳ *Friday*- Throw a couple of pitches to even the littlest batter in the yard or nearby park.

Channel your best *A League of Their Own* character and say very baseball-ey things like:

★ Elbows up!

★ Bend your knees!

★ Keep your eye on the ball!

★ Hey, batter, batter, batter, batter, sa-WING batter!

Courtney Loquasto

April Week 4: Poetry

☀ *Monday* - Introduce some famous children's poets, as well as some books and poems they are known for. Here are a few to get you started:

> ◉ Dr. Seuss (real name Theodore Geisel: 1904-1991)
>
> > ★ *Cat in the Hat* (book)
> > ★ *One Fish, Two Fish, Red Fish, Blue Fish* (book)
> > ★ *The Lorax* (book)
> > ★ *How the Grinch Stole Christmas* (book)
> > ★ *Horton Hatches the Egg* (book)
> > ★ *Fox in Socks* (book)
> > ★ *Green Eggs and Ham* (book)
>
> ◉ Shel Silverstein (1930-1999)
>
> > ★ *Where the Sidewalk Ends* (collection of poems)

- ★ *A Light in the Attic* (collection of poems)
- ★ *The Giving Tree* (book)
- ★ *The Missing Piece* (book)

@ Lewis Carroll (real name Charles Dodgson – author of **Alice's Adventures in Wonderland**, 1832–1898)

- ★ "Beautiful Soup" (poem)
- ★ "How Doth the Little Crocodile" (poem)
- ★ "Jabberwocky" (poem)

@ A.A. Milne (creator of Winnie the Pooh and Christopher Robin, 1882–1956)

- ★ *When We Were Very Young* (collection of poems)
- ★ *Now We Are Six* (collection of poems)
- ★ "At the Zoo" (poem)
- ★ "Us Two" (poem)

@ Louisa May Alcott (author of *Little Women* 1832-1888)

★ "A Song From the Suds" (poem)
★ "Our Little Ghost" (poem)
★ "The Rock and the Bubble" (poem)

See if your child knows the name of any authors of poems. If he can't think of any, see if he can name any authors, period.

If the answer is still no, take a pointer from your grade-school librarian and start to read the author (and illustrator) out loud along with the title when you read books to him.

✳ Tuesday- Play the rhyming game ("I say CAT, you say BAT") for as long as you and he can stand it. If it goes too long, throw out ORANGE.

✳ Wednesday- Introduce Haiku poetry, which is a form of Japanese poetry usually about nature, feelings, or experiences.

The format consists of 3 lines: 5 syllables in the first, 7 syllables in the second, and 5 syllables in the third.

Here's an example of a Haiku poem:

An old silent pond...

A frog jumps into the pond,

Splash! Silence again.

- Basho (1644 -1694)

✳ **Thursday** - Introduce Limericks (which are poems made up of one couplet and one triplet that is usually funny or witty). For example:

There was an old man from Peru,

Who dreamt he was eating his shoe.

He awoke in the night

With a terrible fright

And found out that it was in fact true.

–   Unknown

✳ **Friday** - Have your child take a stab at writing a poem, even if it's a two-liner. If he's too young to write, you can be his writing coach and scribe.

May Week 1: Cinco de Mayo/ Mexico

✷ *Monday*- Explain that Cinco de Mayo is Spanish for *The Fifth of May*.

@ It is an important day in Mexican history because it was when the Mexicans beat the French during a battle in 1862 in the Battle of Puebla.

@ It was a particularly tough fight for the Mexicans. The French had more weapons and more soldiers, similar to what the American soldiers faced in the Revolutionary War.

@ Cinco de Mayo is not celebrated throughout all of Mexico. It is celebrated mostly in the Mexican state where the battle occurred (Puebla) and in the United States.

@ The most important national Mexican holiday is Mexican Independence Day, which is on September 16th. However, now is a good time to introduce your child to some Mexican history and traditions, since Cinco de Mayo is such a popular holiday in the United States.

✳ *Tuesday*- Talk about Mexico's stats:

@ Mexico's official name is **Estados Unidos Mexicanos**, or, the United Mexican States.

@ Mexico's capital city is Mexico City.

@ There are about 110 million people who live in Mexico, which is roughly a third of the size of the United States' population.

@ Mexico's flag is green, white and red. The green represents hope, the white represents purity, and the red represents the blood of the Mexican people. (If you'd rather not say "blood", you can use the word "essence" instead.)

@ The currency of Mexico is the peso.

✳ *Wednesday*- Talk about a few fun things associated with Mexican culture:

@ **Piñatas** are brightly colored, paper mache containers hung up in the air that are filled with candy and toys. Kids whack at the piñata with a stick until it breaks, which sends all of the candy and toys onto the ground for the kids to pick up.

@ **Sombreros** are big, wide brimmed hats made of felt or straw. Some are decorated very ornately, with lots of fringe and sequins. Others are just plain straw. Some people still wear sombreros in Mexico similarly to how some Americans still wear cowboy hats.

@ **A Mariachi band** is a small band of Mexican musicians that usually wear black, silver-studded charro suits and sombreros. They sing about love and play instruments such as trumpets, Spanish guitars and vihuela guitars. Sometimes you can hear them here in the US at Mexican restaurants or Mexican-themed events.

☀ *Thursday* - Mexico is responsible for introducing our country to many of our favorite foods. Here is a list of popular Mexican dishes. See how many your child can name on his own from this list:

★ *Burritos*
★ *Carnitas*
★ *Ceviche*

★ Chile rellenos

★ Enchiladas

★ Flan

★ Fried ice cream

★ Guacamole

★ Pico de gallo

★ Quesadilla

★ Tacos

★ Tamales

★ Tortillas

✳ *Friday* - Review what you talked about this week, and consider taking your family to an authentic Mexican restaurant for lunch or dinner. Do you see any piñatas? The Mexican flag?

Did you *really* get lucky and go on Mariachi band night?

May Week 2: Mother's Day

✳ *Monday* - Ok, this assignment is for the moms:

Help your family out this week! They really *do* want to do something nice for you on Mother's Day, but they may have a hard time correctly figuring out what that something should be.

In the sweetest, subtlest way you know how, tell them what you'd like to receive, be it a real gift, a special meal out together, homemade cards, etc. Make sure you do this today, so they have all week to work with your significant other to make it happen!

✳ *Tuesday* - Tell your child your favorite stories about your own mother, grandmother, great grandmother; as many as you can remember.

✳ *Wednesday* - **Interesting fact**: Anna Jarvis, who had no children herself, is credited with leading the movement that resulted in President Woodrow Wilson signing a Joint Resolution that designated the second Sunday in May as **Mother's Day** in the US in 1914.

She wanted to remember her own mother, who organized women to help wounded solders on both sides of the Civil War.

✱ Thursday- Explain that different species of animals have different lengths of time that they require to grow a baby. Look at how varied the gestation lengths are!

- ★ Humans: 9 months
- ★ Hamsters: 16 days
- ★ Lions: 108 days
- ★ Whales: about a year (360 days)
- ★ Indian Elephants: about 1 year 9 months (624 days)

✱ Friday- Make sure you have lots of art supplies in locations that are in plain sight. Little hands might need to access them quickly to make a Mother's Day card tonight!

Or, realistically, early Sunday morning (*wink).

May Week 3: Planting a Raised Garden

※ *Monday* - Work with your child to budget for some gardening supplies later this week. Allowance money works just fine here.

Take stock of who has what and who needs what (gloves, shovels, garden trowels, dirt, compost, seeds, wood). Start a working list for the store.

※ *Tuesday* - Talk about what you want to plant this year with your family.

Remember to include your significant other in this conversation, as there is a good chance he or she will be asked to participate this weekend!

※ *Wednesday* - Go outside and pick a spot for your garden, paying special attention to how flat it is and when (and if) it gets sun. Morning sun is bright and less intense; afternoon sun is hot and often humid.

Point out the difference between sunny spots and shady spots out to your child and see if he can figure out which tree/ bush/ house is making the shade.

Take a picture of the spot where you'd like to have the garden, then do some consensus building in your house.

✳ *Thursday* - Today is your big day at the store to get your garden supplies!

This can be a very expensive or very inexpensive project, depending on what bells and whistles you choose for your garden.

Either way, don't forget to pull up the store's website to see if they have any coupons or special offers on what you're about to buy.

While shopping for seeds and/ or potted plants, read the directions for planting on each. Make sure you pick varieties that are intended for the type of sun your garden will get (morning or afternoon, full or shade).

✳ *Friday* - Review your garden plan with your entire family and get busy creating your very own raised garden this weekend.

Happy Planting!

May Week 4: Kites

✷ *Monday* - - Kites have played important roles throughout history. Some famous kite flyers:

- ℮ **Ben Franklin**, who used a kite in an experiment to see if lightning was electricity,
- ℮ **Alexander Graham Bell**, who is most famous for inventing the telephone, but who also built kites to help out with the "flying machine problem", (which was the fact that the modern airplane had not been invented yet), and
- ℮ **The Wright Brothers**, who used kites in the development of the first airplane.

✷ *Tuesday* - Talk about some different types of kites:

- ★ Diamond kite (shaped like a diamond)
- ★ Delta Kite (shaped like the Greek alphabet Delta symbol, which looks like a triangle)

★ Box kite (shaped like a box and open at both ends)

★ Dragon kite (a kite train, or a chain of individual kites, each with its own tether).

✳ Wednesday – If it's been a while since you yourself have flown a kite, here is a little refresher guide to help you get the kite in the air:

1. Check the weather for wind speed. 5 to 15 mile per hour winds are good for kite flying.

2. Find a large, open space free of power lines and trees.

3. Let out about 15 feet of string.

4. Hand the spool to your little one, (if you're sure it's a good idea).

5. Notice which way the wind is blowing, and face him against the wind.

6. Stand behind him, holding the kite up.

7. Now say, "Run!" and follow him until you let go and the kite takes flight.

8. Catch up to him, take the spool, and let the string out gradually, sending the kite higher and higher into the sky.

9. Show him how to tug the spool up and down to keep the kite in the sky.

10.   Hand the spool back to him.

11.   Stay close, in case the wind changes suddenly; that kite will be coming down like a rocket headed straight for Earth! (Also, pay close attention that the kite string stays clear of little necks.)

✳ *Thursday*- Take a trip to Target, a drugstore, grocery, etc. and buy a $3 kite. Now find a big open space and fly it. (Remember to keep the string away from power lines and necks!)

**I realize that's the second week in the row I've asked you to go out and spend money, but, hopefully both of these investments will last you all summer and be well worth the money you spend on them.

✳ *Friday*- Skip the review and fly the kite again.

You are the parent, after all, so it's not considered slacking when you suggest it!

Courtney Loquasto

June Week 1: Bugs

✳ *Monday* - - Explain that bees have to pollinate 2000 flowers to make one tablespoon of honey.

If you have honey on hand, you could pour out 1 tablespoon of honey to demonstrate how small an amount that is for such a large amount of flowers.

✳ *Tuesday* - The biggest spider in the world is the Goliath Bird-Eating Tarantula. It has a leg span of a foot (when fully extended).

If you have a ruler handy, it might help to point out how long a foot is, so your child can picture the enormity of this spider.

Don't worry – it only lives in South America.

✳ *Wednesday* - Glass jelly jars make good bug-watching containers for children that are old enough to respect and handle glass.

Just wash out the jar, then take the lid and lay it flat on top of a thick piece of scrap wood. Hammer in (and remove) a nail 5 or 6 times through the lid to create breathing holes.

Put a few pieces of grass and sticks in there and you have a nice bug habitat.

Do remember, though: If your child chooses bugs that are smaller than the air holes, those bugs are coming out.

Soon.

✳ Thursday- **Interesting fact**: There was a bug that lived on Earth even before the dinosaurs.

The Archimylacris Eggintoni (the cockroach's ancestor) was around 300 million years ago, which was about 50 million years before the dinosaurs.

✳ Friday- Review what you talked about this week and check on the bugs in the jar.

June Week 2: Father's Day

✳ *Monday* - America's Founding Fathers were the political leaders who played key roles in the American Revolution and established the new nation after independence was won (specifically by developing the Declaration of Independence and the US Constitution).

In words little ones can understand, they were "the first guys in our country to come up with our government".

Although the list of the Founding Fathers is not technically official, here are the men many people agree on:

★ George Washington
★ Ben Franklin
★ Thomas Jefferson
★ John Adams
★ James Madison
★ Samuel Adams
★ Alexander Hamilton.

❋ Tuesday - Tell the story about what your husband/ you did when each child was born. Make sure you don't leave out any details, and get ready to repeat the story approximately seven to thirty-seven times.

❋ Wednesday - This one's for the moms again: Have your child make a Father's Day gift.

If your child is very young, hold the crayon in his hands. If he is bigger, try to help him put together something that is heartfelt and specific to what your husband/significant other likes.

As part of the gift, you could have your child brainstorm his favorite memories with his dad. If he can't write yet, be his scribe, then roll the paper up and tie it with a string like a treasure map.

If you *are* the dad, start planting notes like "Make Dad Father's Day Things" in high-traffic family areas.

❋ Thursday - Moms: Have your child help you plan and make a special meal for your husband/significant other on Sunday. This means he helps make the shopping list, shops with you, and then helps you make any preparations necessary ahead of the day itself. Again, if you're the father, you could casually mention what your favorite meal is, whether it fits into the conversation or not. You truly *do* want to help them get this right, after all...

✳ *Friday*- A brief history lesson on Father's Day:

While Mother's Day became a national holiday in 1914, it wasn't until ten years later that President Calvin Coolidge nationally recognized Father's Day. It was originally recommended by Sonora Louise Smart Dodd, one of six children, who was raised by her father.

Sonora's dad was a Civil War veteran and farmer. Her mother died giving birth to her sixth child when Sonora was 16. Sonora was the only daughter in the family, and she helped her father raise her younger brothers, including the baby.

Sonora heard about the new holiday, Mother's Day, in church. She loved and respected her own father very much, and took it upon herself to campaign for an official Father's Day. She suggested it be on June 5th, her father's birthday, but her city government chose what we still use today: the third Sunday in June.

Courtney Loquasto

June Week 3: Swimming

☀ *Monday* - The 4 basic strokes of swimming are:

1. Freestyle

2. Breaststroke

3. Butterfly

4. Backstroke

5. (And don't forget the unofficial #5: the Doggie-Paddle).

☀ *Tuesday* - Share your favorite story involving a pool, lake, or the ocean.

If you're not a fan of swimming in the water, talk about something you do like about it (even if it's sitting in a hot tub.)

☀ *Wednesday* - **Interesting fact**: Bathing suits have changed a lot. In the early 1900's, men and women wore long pants, skirts and shirts to the beach.

The bikini debuted in 1946.

✳ *Thursday* - **Another interesting fact**: Michael Phelps, an American Olympic swimmer, won 8 gold medals in the 2008 Beijing Olympics, which is currently the record for most gold medals won in a single Olympics.[1]

✳ *Friday* - Teach some swimming moves out of the water, like what to do with your arms for the different types of swimming strokes that you are familiar with, or how to do a scissor kick (you can demonstrate by laying on your back on the floor).

Hint: You may want to do this away from the windows.

---

[1] As of 2012

June Week 4: The ABC's

☀ *Monday* - If you have a little-little guy, work on the alphabet song.

If you have a bigger kid, have him write as much of the ABC's in print, uppercase, lowercase, and/ or cursive as he can.

If you have an even bigger kid, have him write a word or sentence that starts with each letter of the alphabet. Wish him luck with "X"!

☀ *Tuesday* - Take turns playing this sing-songy game with your child:

The letter A goes like this:

> A My name is Alice and my
> (husband/significant other's) name
> is Albert and I come from
> Albuquerque and I - love -Apples!"

Then for B:

B My name is Burt and my wife's name is Betty and I come from Boston and I love Bananas!''

The same goes for C, and so on.

❋ *Wednesday* People who are blind can use their fingers to read Braille (a system of raised dots on stiff paper that was developed by a French educator who lost his sight at the age of three).

The Braille alphabet looks like this:

Braille Alphabet:

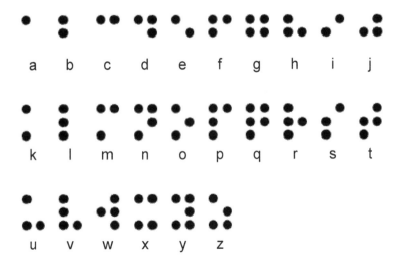

✻ *Thursday*- People who are deaf can use sign language to communicate. The sign language alphabet looks like this: 2

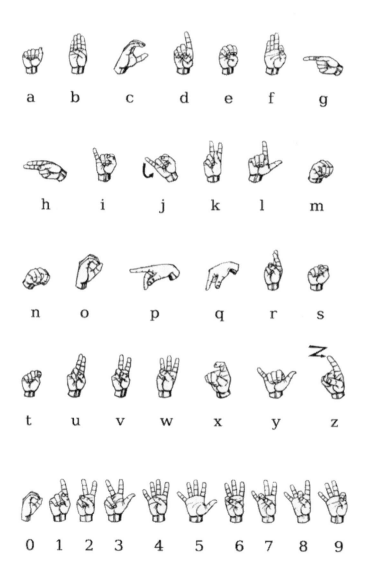

2 ASL Alphabet Chart, from pdclipart.org, a public domain clip art site

❋ *Friday* - Review what you talked about this week, and see if your kid(s) remember any of the Braille or sign language letters.

July Week 1: America

✳ *Monday* - Explain that, in the United States, the person we commonly give credit to discovering America is the Italian explorer Christopher Columbus, in 1492.

However, according to Icelandic literature (called the **Sagas of Icelanders**), it was the explorer Leif Eriksson who first discovered our continent, about 500 years before Columbus.

He was on his way home to Greenland from Norway and got caught in a storm. He accidentally ended up in what is now Canada. He called it *Vineland* because it had so many grape vines.

✳ *Tuesday* - Teach your child our national anthem, "The Star Spangled Banner" by Francis Scott Key.

Explain that he wrote the song after he saw the American flag still standing after the British attacked Fort McHenry in the War of 1812:

Oh say, can you see by the dawn's early
light,

What so proudly we hailed at the
twilight's last gleaming?

Whose broad stripes and bright stars
through the perilous fight,

O'er the ramparts we watched, were so
gallantly streaming?
And the rockets' red glare, the bombs
bursting in air,

Gave proof through the night that our
flag was still there;

Oh, say does that star-spangled banner
yet wave,

O'er the land of the free and the home
of the brave?

✳ Wednesday Interesting fact: The wingspan
of our national bird, the bald eagle, is from about 5.5
to 7.5 feet. Point out where your own height falls in
that range, to give your child some perspective about
how big that is.

✳ Thursday - Explain that we watch fireworks, have parades, carnivals and BBQ's in the USA on July 4th to celebrate our adoption of the Declaration of Independence (from Britain, in 1776).

✳ Friday - Here's an easy, patriotic art project to make an American flag:

1. Cut 13 horizontal stripes from a piece of red construction paper.

2. Glue onto a white piece of paper as horizontal stripes (red stripe at the top and bottom).

3. Cut out a blue rectangle, ¼ of a blue sheet of construction paper.

4. Glue to the top left side of the flag.

5. Using a white crayon, white chalk, or little white star stickers, create 9 offset horizontal rows of stars in the blue rectangle, with the following pattern from the top: 6 stars, 5 stars, 6, 5, 6, 5, 6, 5, 6, for a pretty darn authentic-looking American flag.

Courtney Loquasto

July Week 2: The Library

✳ *Monday* - **Interesting fact**: The first public US library was set up by Ben Franklin in 1731, and it was called ***The Library Company of Philadelphia.***

✳ *Tuesday* - Explain that the Dewey Decimal System is a way libraries organize books into categories, which makes it easy to find books and return them to their proper place.

Point out the Dewey Decimal number on a library book you have at home, or on the books the next time you visit the library.

✳ *Wednesday* - What can you check out at the library anymore? Every library is different, but it's not just books and tapes. Some libraries now offer:

★ eBooks
★ Downloadable movies
★ Downloadable audiobooks
★ Streaming videos

- ★ MP3 CDs
- ★ DVDs
- ★ Podcasts
- ★ CDs
- ★ Books on CDs
- ★ Children's read-alongs (book with cassette)
- ★ Musical scores

And of course, rows and rows of delicious plastic wrapped-books just waiting for you and your child to explore!

What's the best part of the library? It is still absolutely free (as long as you don't lose what you borrow, in which case it becomes rather expensive, especially since you then own the book you can't find).

✹ Thursday- Take a trip to the library and check out lots of books.

If you are able, get everyone their own library card, and make a big, hairy deal about it. Maybe you can re-use an old wallet of yours and provide a special place for your child to keep his very important card.

✹ Friday- Ask your child which library book is his favorite so far, and have him give you a book report (as best he can for his age) about the setting, main character, and plot of the story.

Courtney Loquasto

July Week 3: The Ocean

✳ *Monday* - Explain that about 72% of the Earth is covered with water, and almost all (97%) of it is found in the oceans.

A good way to demonstrate this is to take an apple or orange and cover just about ¾ of it with your hands.

✳ *Tuesday* - Share the quote:

Water, water everywhere, nor any drop to drink

from the poem "The Rime of the Ancient Mariner" by the English poet Samuel Taylor Coleridge.

Humans can't drink seawater because it is too salty. We would become dehydrated if we drank it and end up more thirsty than when we started.

✳ *Wednesday* - There are approximately 250,000 known marine species in the ocean.. Have your kid(s) (and you) name as many things as you can that live in the ocean.

✳ **Thursday** - Some surfer nicknames for different kinds of waves include:

- ★ Avalanche
- ★ Bluebird
- ★ Beach break
- ★ Clean up
- ★ Close out
- ★ Double up
- ★ Hollow
- ★ Left
- ★ Outside
- ★ Point break
- ★ Reef break
- ★ Tube
- ★ Zipper

✳ **Friday** - Have some fish for dinner, and be sure to mention what type it is. See how many other names of fish that your family eats you all can come up with.

(This would probably not be a good day to watch *Finding Nemo*.)

July Week 4: Friends

☀ *Monday* - Teach your child the song/ phrase "Make New Friends but Keep the Old" (Author Unknown). Here are the first few verses:

Make new friends,

But keep the old.

One is silver,

The other is gold.

A circle is round,

It has no end.

That's how long,

I will be your friend.

A fire burns bright,

It warms your heart.

We've been friends,

From the very start.

You have one hand,

I have the other,

Put them together,

We have each other.

✳ **Tuesday**- Have your child tell you all about each of his friends. Have him talk about his favorite quality in each one.

✳ **Wednesday**-Many little issues young kids have with their friends can be solved with empathy (easily explained as "putting yourself in someone else's shoes").

Talk about a time when your child was either on the giving or receiving end of a situation where someone got their feelings hurt.

Talk through how putting ourselves in someone else's shoes helps us to understand why people do the things they do, or why they get their feelings hurt when we didn't mean to hurt them.

✳ **Thursday**- List off some famous fictional friends your young child might recognize.

An older kid may have to wrack his brain a little to remember some of these (which could be fun to watch!)

Say the first name in the pair and see if your child can name the other(s):

- ★ Clifford the Big Red Dog and Emily
- ★ Huck Finn and Tom Sawyer
- ★ Batman and Robin
- ★ Bert and Ernie
- ★ Curious George and the Man with the Yellow Hat
- ★ Lowly Worm and Huckle Cat
- ★ Charlie Brown and Snoopy
- ★ Bonus: can they name all four? Anthony, Murray, Jeff, Sam or Greg (the Wiggles)

✳ **Friday**- Have your child make a card, draw a picture or write a letter for a friend who is sad, sick or who lives far away.

As he is creating his project, tell him what Charles Dickens' said about having friends:

Friendship? Yes, please.

August Week 1: Picnics

✳ *Monday* - Together, list out loud some good things to bring on a picnic:

- ★ Apples
- ★ Bananas
- ★ Book of jokes
- ★ Bug spray
- ★ Camera
- ★ Carrots
- ★ Celery
- ★ Chocolate-chip cookies
- ★ Drinks
- ★ Eating utensils
- ★ Games
- ★ Grapes
- ★ Hats
- ★ Napkins
- ★ Picnic blanket
- ★ Sandwiches
- ★ Sun block

★ Trash Bag

★ Watermelon

★ Wet-wipes

✹ Tuesday- **Interesting fact**: The reason ants are such a problem for picnickers is because once they find you, they leave a scent for the other ants to follow to get to you and your food. Thus, the line of ants to your watermelon.

✹ Wednesday-Another interesting fact: The sandwich is named after John Montagu, the 4th Earl of Sandwich in England (1718-1792).

✹ Thursday- Talk about some good shady trees to sit under. Here are a few types commonly found in the U.S.:

★ Birch

★ Elm

★ Maple

★ Oak

✹ Friday- Have your child help you pack and eat a picnic lunch or breakfast outside.

If it's raining, have a picnic inside on a blanket in a place you don't usually eat, like your living room.

August Week 2: Butterflies

✹ *Monday* Talk about the different stages of the butterfly life cycle, which are:

1. Egg

2. Larva (caterpillar)

3. Pupa (chrysalis)

4. Butterfly

✹ *Tuesday* **Interesting facts**: The top butterfly flight speed is 12 miles per hour, and the wingspan of the largest butterflies can be up to 12 inches.

✹ *Wednesday* **Another interesting fact:** Caterpillars eat plants, but butterflies drink nectar from flowers, sap from trees and sugars from rotting fruit with the long tube in their mouth that they use like a straw.

If you're hoping to watch some butterflies, plant some big, bright flowers in your raised garden.

✳ *Thursday* - If you (or your child, if he's braver than you) would like to catch a butterfly, spray your (or his) hand with sugar water, and stand near a spot with lots of flowers.

A butterfly might just come and sit on your or his hand.

✳ *Friday* - Does everyone know what a butterfly kiss is? It's a kiss you give someone by batting your eyelashes right up next to their eyelashes. It's extremely tickly and fun.

Make sure you mention to your child that a butterfly kiss is only to be given to a person he is very close to, or even just family, unless you want that uncomfortable phone call from his teacher that makes you feel like you're raising Don Juan (or Don Draper).

August Week 3: School

✱ *Monday* - What level of school is next for your child? What do you remember from that stage in life? Share your stories to demystify the unknown a little for him.

✱ *Tuesday* - Talk about what new school supplies your child will need this year, and make a shopping list together.

If he's not enrolled in school yet, you can still plan for your school year of Little Lesson Plans. After all, everybody likes a new pack of crayons, even you (busted!)

✱ *Wednesday* - Go over any big changes your child has coming this year. Is he waking up earlier? Changing classes? Eating lunch at school? Talk through what each change will mean to him and come up with a plan together to help him handle the change.

✱ *Thursday* - Is your child going to be riding the bus for the first time? If so, talk about what to expect (a nice bus driver, sitting next to kids in the neighborhood, friendly teachers waiting to tell him where to go when he gets to school, etc.)

If he doesn't ride the bus yet (or never will), point it out when you see it drive by like it's a big, exciting, special occasion.

And if riding the bus is old-hat for your kid, have him come up with a friendly nickname for his bus this year, and have your whole family stick with it.

Here are some example bus nicknames to get you started:

★ Big Bertha

★ The Big Cheese, or

★ The Wagon of Wonder

✸ *Friday* - (Advice from my former-schoolteacher Mom): Remember, your child looks to you on how to respond to things in his world. Your attitude toward school is going to greatly influence what set of eyes he sees his school experience through.

@ If you act nervous about school, he will walk in under a cloud of worry himself.

@ If you thought school was a pain and let him know it, he will go in each day thinking school is a pain as well, and it may very quickly become one for him.

🌀 But if you act excited about school, he will
anticipate that something great will be
waiting for him each day. Based on his
attitude alone, it probably will be.

Courtney Loquasto

August Week 4: Money

✳ *Monday* - Review different types of US currency-
the dollar, quarter, dime, nickel and penny.

If you have a little-little guy, consider a look-but-
don't-touch situation.

You may want to give an older child a little math
quiz (two quarters plus a dime plus a nickel equals
how much? Whose face appears on which coin?) and
let him keep the change for the right answer.

✳ *Tuesday* - There was a famous study done by
Walter Mischel of Stanford in the late sixties called
the "Marshmallow Test". During the test, he offered
4 to 6 year-olds one marshmallow right away, or, if
they could do it, two marshmallows after a short
wait.

Only 1/3 of them were able to wait and receive the
two marshmallows.

A follow up study indicated there was a strong
correlation between those kids who were able to wait

135

for the two marshmallows and higher SAT scores, less behavioral problems, and more general successes in their lives.3

Knowing this, see how your own child does with a test of delayed gratification.

- @ When you're at the store again, offer him the opportunity to pick out a toy that costs one dollar at the beginning of the shopping trip or, if he can wait, a toy that costs two dollars at the end of the shopping trip (or two toys that cost one dollar each).

- @ Depending on what he chooses, tell him (in terms appropriate for his age) about the study. Re-emphasize that it is a good thing to have self control and to be able to find a way to have the situation work for him, especially when it comes to money.

- @ Don't be discouraged if your child picks the one dollar treat. Self control, to some degree, depends on age and maturity (and you can *teach* it, like you're doing now!)

---

3 From the article "Don't! The Secret of Self Control" by Jonah Lehrer, appearing in *The New Yorker* May 18, 2009

✳ **Wednesday**-Sit down with the whole family and decide if you are ready to adopt an allowance system. Questions to consider:

- Are you going to have a set of jobs that must be completed for payout each week?

- Is it an all-or-nothing scenario? For example, must you do all of the jobs listed to get the allowance (not just some of them)?

- Are you going to have a special list of jobs that payout right away?

- Are you going to pay once a week, twice a week, once a month, etc?

- How much money will you pay, or will you use a different incentive?

- Is the allowance going to be different for each child in your family?

- What percentage of each dollar are the kids expected to:

  - ★ Save
  - ★ Give (to charity, church, etc.)
  - ★ Spend?

✳ *Thursday*- Have your child help you make a piggy bank for everyone in the house who is not going to eat the coins.

Coffee cans with soft plastic lids are great, just cut a rectangle the size of the side of a matchbox in the lid and have your child decorate the sides of the can with construction paper and stickers.

✳ *Friday*- Do some of the chores you've assigned for allowance alongside with your child, in order to demonstrate:

- ★ The correct way to do them
- ★ Where everything is stored
- ★ That doing housework is a whole, whole lot of fun, right, Mommy/ Daddy? (Wink-wink).

September Week 1: Grandparents

✳ *Monday*- Talk about how Grandparents' Day became a holiday:

Marian McQuade, a housewife from Virginia, championed the idea of making a national holiday to benefit the elderly in nursing homes. In 1978, President Jimmy Carter made Grandparents Day official, to be celebrated the first Sunday after Labor day every year.

✳ *Tuesday*- Have your child come up with a list of questions on his own of things he'd like to know about his grandparents. Some question ideas:

- ★ Where were they born?
- ★ How did they meet?
- ★ Where was their favorite place to live?
- ★ Do they like ice cream?

If his grandparents are living, have him interview them in person. If they are deceased, you and your spouse/ significant other can answer the questions as best you can for them.

✻ *Wednesday* Have your child write a generic letter or draw a picture about grandparents and drop it off at a local nursing home.

You could ask a staff member to give it to the person who needs it the most that day.

✻ *Thursday* Make a list of each of your child's traits that have been attributed to a grandparent. For example:

> ★ Eyes = Grandpa on Dad's side
> ★ Nose = Grandma on Mom's side

Read the list out loud at dinner to see if anyone can come up with any others.

✻ *Friday* Make Grandparent's Day cards for all living grandparents (ahhh, but you *knew* that was coming, right?)

September Week 2: Planets and Stars

✺ *Monday* - Explain that the sun is the center of our solar system, and all of the planets revolve around it.

You can demonstrate this by circling a little ball around a much bigger ball, to show the general motion and comparison of the sun vs. the planets (though this demonstration isn't even close to scale - You could fit about 960,000 Earths into the sun.)

✺ *Tuesday* - Talk about the planets of our solar system in order from the sun. Remember:

My Very Excellent Mother Just Served Us Nine Pizzas?

Well, now she serves us only nachos! Pluto is currently classified by NASA as a dwarf planet.

So, here is today's updated list of planets:

★ Mercury

★ Venus

- ★ Earth
- ★ Mars
- ★ Jupiter
- ★ Saturn
- ★ Uranus
- ★ Neptune

❋ **Wednesday**– **Interesting fact:** The moon revolves around the earth and helps to stabilize our climate.

Relatively speaking, you could fit about 4 moons into one earth.

❋ **Thursday**- Explain that Mars appears red because it is made up largely of iron oxide, or, as we know it, rust.

NASA has had 2 twin robots on Mars since January 2004 collecting and analyzing the rocks and soil. They've taken lots of very cool pictures of the surface of Mars (that can be seen in various books published on the topic, as well as on www.NASA.gov).

❋ **Friday**- Review what you talked about this week while you lay on your backs and gaze at the stars, if your kid is allowed to be up that late (or early).

Give it at least 15 minutes and you might even see a shooting star (which is actually, most likely, a piece of space trash entering the atmosphere. But who cares – it's still awesome).

Courtney Loquasto

September Week 3: Trees

❋ *Monday* - **Interesting fact**: If you look at the
tree stump of a tree that has fallen on its own or been
cut down, you can see the rings inside the trunk.

Each ring represents one year of the tree's life. Fatter
rings were good years with lots of water, thinner
rings were drier years.

❋ *Tuesday* - *How to press pretty Fall leaves:*

> **1.** Collect different leaves that have fallen on the
> ground and lay the dry ones (without mold)
> flat, inside two pieces of newspaper.

> **2.** Lay a couple of big, heavy books on top of the
> papers and we'll come back to these
> tomorrow.

❋ *Wednesday* - Take the pressed leaves out from
the newspaper and have your child glue his favorite
ones to construction paper.

With it, make a Fall greeting card for someone with a
birthday around this time of year, or for someone
who might be lonely.

✳ **Thursday - Another interesting fact:**

Deciduous trees lose their leaves in the colder weather, and then grow new leaves when the warmer weather comes back.

Conifers (or evergreens) lose their leaves or needles a little bit all year round, so it appears that they always have them, or are "forever green".

✳ **Friday - Some tree jokes:**

@ What is a tree's least favorite month?

Sep-timber

@ What do you call a tree that can fit in your hand?

A palm tree

@ What did the beaver say to the tree?

It's been nice gnawing you

September Week 4: Musical Instruments

✳ *Monday* - A musical instrument is anything that can be used to make a musical tone or sound.

Have your child brainstorm different things that could be used as a musical instrument, from the conventional (drum, violin, piano, etc.) to the creative (nose, kazoo, water dripping, rubber band snapping, etc).

✳ *Tuesday* - Talk about the different categories we generally group musical instruments into:

- ★ Brass (tuba, trumpet, etc)
- ★ Keyboard (piano)
- ★ Percussion (drums, bells)
- ★ String (violin, guitar) and
- ★ Woodwind (flute, clarinets)

If you have any instruments at home (child or adult versions) bring them out, talk about what group they belong to, and have your child try each out.

If you don't have any instruments, flip a pot upside down and whack it with a spoon for a makeshift drum.

✳ *Wednesday* There are many different types of music.

See if your child can name any of these genres from the following list:

- ★ Big Band/ Swing
- ★ Blues
- ★ Christian
- ★ Classical
- ★ Country
- ★ Dance
- ★ Disco
- ★ Folk
- ★ Hip Hop
- ★ Jazz
- ★ Pop
- ★ Reggae
- ★ Rock

Play different types of songs on the radio, satellite/internet stations, Itunes, TV stations, etc. See if your child can name the type of music he's hearing.

Point out the differences in the music to help him decipher what type of music it is, like the slower vs. faster beats, different instruments used, and how the song is sung (if there's a vocalist).

❋ *Thursday* - Reading sheet music 101: Even if your child has never taken any sort of music class, you can help him remember which notes are on a treble clef staff (the most common clef used today) with the following mnemonic devices:

@ For the notes on the lines:

<u>E</u>very <u>G</u>ood <u>B</u>oy <u>D</u>oes <u>F</u>ine

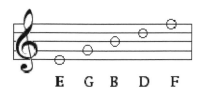

E   G   B   D   F

@ And for the notes in the spaces in-between:

F-A-C-E

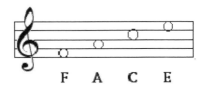

It may not make sense to him yet, but by the time he gets into his first music class, he will already have these phrases stored away, ready for use when it's time.

✳ *Friday* - Did you know the song "Do-Re-Mi" from ***The Sound of Music*** by Rodgers and Hammerstein is actually training for how to sing a C scale?

Each of the syllables sung is on pitch to represent one of the eight notes scale. The syllables for each note are:

★ *Do (C)*
★ *Re (D)*
★ *Mi (E)*
★ *Fa (F)*
★ *Sol (G)*
★ *La (A)*
★ *Ti (B)*
★ *(Do) (C)*

October Week 1: Cars, Trucks, Planes and Trains

* ☀ *Monday*- **Interesting fact**: Monster trucks use a type of tires called Terra tires, which are 66 inches tall and 43 inches wide.

  That's probably close to as tall as you (66 inches is 5 foot 5 inches) and wider than your refrigerator.

* ☀ *Tuesday*- **More interesting facts**: As of 2012, the fastest train in the world is in China, and can go 302 miles per hour.

  Big passenger airplanes cruise at around 500 miles per hour.

* ☀ *Wednesday*- (This is a gross one, but the boys should love it): Before cars were invented, there was the great Horse Manure Crisis of 1894.

Because all modes of transportation in cities were pulled by horses, the fact that they produce between 15 and 35 pounds of manure a day was becoming quite a problem. The people were running out of places to put the horses' – ehem - stuff.

There was even an international conference held in NYC in 1898 to discuss the situation, but the delegates quit after 3 days instead of the planned 10, because nobody could figure out a good solution. The situation seemed hopeless.

Luckily, Henry Ford figured out how to mass produce automobiles shortly thereafter, and the horse manure crisis was solved, just in time.

✻ **Thursday** - Some entertaining trucker lingo:

> ★ Alligator = blown tire in the road
> ★ Bear = police officer
> ★ Bikini state = Florida
> ★ Salt shaker = snow plow
> ★ Wiggle wagon = double trailer truck

✻ **Friday** - Review what you talked about this week, and point out Wiggle Wagons, Alligators, Bears and Salt Shakers when you're on the roads.

And don't forget to take a moment to appreciate Mr. Henry Ford for solving the problem you talked about on Wednesday!

October Week 2: Apples

✹ *Monday* - Talk about the most common types of apples and their characteristics:

- ★ **Braeburn** (red, firm, juicy, slightly tart)
- ★ **Fuji** (dark red with small light colored dots, large, crunchy, sweet)
- ★ **Gala** (light red with yellow streaks, juicy, not very crunchy)
- ★ **Golden Delicious** (yellow, sweet, thin skin)
- ★ **Granny Smith** (green, sour, hard flesh)
- ★ **Gravenstein** (reddish-green, thin skin, juicy, tart)
- ★ **McIntosh** (red, round, white flesh, spicy)
- ★ **Red Delicious** (dark red, 5 knobs on the bottom)

✹ *Tuesday* - Tell your child about Johnny Appleseed, the nickname given to the American

155

pioneer John Chapman (1774-1845), who introduced apple trees to parts of Ohio, Indiana and Illinois.

His dream was to grow so many apples that no one would ever go hungry. Legend has it he carried a bag with apple seeds that he got for free from cider mills and planted apple seeds everywhere he went.

✻ *Wednesday* How to plant your own apple tree at home:

1. Save some seeds from an apple you liked.

2. Place the seeds out to dry.

3. Once they are completely dry, place them in a wet paper towel and put the paper towel with the seeds inside in a sandwich bag.

4. Put the bag in the fridge.

5. After about 4-5 weeks, see if any of the seeds have sprouted.

6. If they have, move the sprouts to a small pot of soil and place in a sunny window.

7. Keep moving the seedlings to bigger pots as they grow, and water them often.

8. You can move the saplings from their pot to the outdoors once the threat of frost is over for the year.

Though, actually the ideal time to plant the tree(s) in the ground will be next fall, right after all the leaves have fallen off the trees around you.

Make sure you plant it where it can get plenty of sun (12 hours a day), and water it often. It should start producing apples in as early as three years.

✳ *Thursday*- Trivia for your child:

> *What city is nicknamed "The Big Apple"?*
> *Answer: New York City.*

✳ *Friday*- Bring your child with you to the store to pick out some apples.

See what varieties are in season and for sale where you live, and, using your recently acquired apple knowledge, pick out the ones that sound the tastiest.

Courtney Loquasto

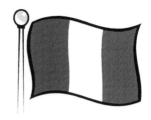

October Week 3: Columbus Day / Italy

✳ *Monday* - Christopher Columbus, the Italian explorer mentioned in our *America* section in July, was looking for a direct sea route from Europe to Asia, when he accidentally discovered America.

The Spanish Queen, Isabella I, paid for his trip.

✳ *Tuesday* - Talk about how Italy is a peninsula (a large mass of land that extends into a body of water) and is shaped like a boot.

✳ *Wednesday* -**Interesting facts**: The first modern pizza was invented by baker Raffaele Esposito in Naples, Italy around 1860.

Today, October is National Pizza Month in the United States. Over 5 billion pizzas are sold worldwide each year, and 3 billion of those are sold in the US.

Mangiare! (Pronounced "Mahn-jah"- Italian for *eat.*)

✳ *Thursday-* Famous Italian inventors and their inventions:

- ★ Galileo Galilei- the telescope
- ★ Aldus Manutius- cursive handwriting
- ★ Allessandro Volta- the electric battery
- ★ Bartolomeo Cristofori- the piano

✳ *Friday-* Review what you talked about this week, and how about making some Italian Gravy (slow-cooked tomato sauce) for dinner, with or without the meatballs?

October Week 4: Halloween

※ *Monday*- Who is the spookiest poet of all? Why, Edgar Allen Poe, of course! Here is an ominous verse from his famous poem "The Raven":

Once upon a midnight dreary, while I pondered, weak and weary,

Over many a quaint and curious volume of forgotten lore,

While I nodded, nearly napping, suddenly there came a tapping,

As of some one gently rapping, rapping at my chamber door.

"Tis some visitor," I muttered, "tapping at my chamber door-

Only this and nothing more.

...or was it? *Mwwah-ha-ha-ha-ha...*

✳ *Tuesday* - How to roast pumpkin seeds:

1. Right after you carve a pumpkin, rinse the seeds in a colander with cold water and throw away the strings and goop.

2. Lay the seeds on a kitchen towel and pat off excess water.

3. Put the seeds on a baking sheet lightly oiled with olive oil (about ½ teaspoon), and stir the seeds around to coat them in the oil.

4. Sprinkle a little sea salt over all of the seeds and bake at 325° for about 25 minutes, or until golden brown.

5. Store in an airtight container.

✳ *Wednesday* -Some Halloween jokes:

@ *What do you get when you cross Bambi with a ghost?*

Bam-boo

@ *What does a ghost eat for lunch?*

Boo-logna sandwiches

@ Where do ghosts mail their letters?

The ghost office

@ How do you fix a broken Jack-o-lantern?

With a pumpkin patch

@ What do you call a witch that lives at the beach?

A sand-witch

✳ Thursday - Here's a fun song for Halloween that can double as an anatomy lesson:

Dem Dry Bones

(Traditional Spiritual, author unknown)

The toe bone connected to the heel bone.

The heel bone connected to the foot bone.

The foot bone connected to the ankle bone.

It's easy to connect those dry bones.

The foot bone connected to the leg bone.

The leg bone connected to the knee bone.

The knee bone connected to the thigh bone.

It's easy to connect those dry bones.

✳ *Friday* - Practice the jokes. They will come in handy if you are scheduled to be a trick-or-treating chaperone or stay-at-home candy-slinger.

November Week 1: U.S. Government / Elections

✳ *Monday* - Talk about how the US government is broken into 3 branches:

1. **Legislative** (House of Representatives and Congress)
2. **Executive** (President and Vice President)
3. **Judicial** (the Supreme Court)

If you have a little-little guy, it may entertain you to just try to have them pronounce the words. Especially *judicial*.

Explain that our Founding Fathers set up our government in this way so that no one person would have too much power.

Each branch of our government can check the powers of the other two in order to maintain a balance of authority, which is what we call *checks and balances.*

✳ **T*uesday*** - Is it a mid-term or election year? Your daily assignment is to vote!

✳ **W*ednesday*** - Explain that the US is a democracy. This means the people of our country elect (or decide) who is in office.

Some other countries are autocracies, which means they are run by one person, sometimes without the consent of the people in that country.

Every person in the US that is 18 years old or older and is a legal citizen gets to vote.

✳ **T*hursday*** - Tell your child that we vote for:

@ **President/Vice President** every 4 years (2012, 2016, 2020, etc)

@ One-third of the **Senate** every 2 years (Senators serve a 6-year term)

@ **Representatives** every 2 years (though not everyone who is eligible in the state votes for the representatives. Only the people that live in the congressional district that the candidate will represent do)

✳ *Friday* - Talk to your child about what it's like to vote. If he's ever gone with you, he's probably very interested in what you've been doing behind that curtain!

Courtney Loquasto

November Week 2: Charity

✳ *Monday* - Explain to your child that charity means opening your heart and giving in some way to someone in need. It doesn't have to mean giving money or things.

Talk to your child about the gifts God gave him. What does he consider gifts of his that are special to just him? A good voice, a nice smile, or good at telling jokes? Make a list of what he comes up with.

Go down the list and brainstorm with him how he can share his gifts with someone else.

> ★ *Can he sing in the choir?*
> ★ *Can he try to smile and say 'hello' to an elderly person in a store?*
> ★ *Can he tell his jokes to a friend of his who is sad?*

✳ *Tuesday* - If your child is receiving allowance, ask him to come up with a plan to do something special with his money for someone else.

If he has trouble coming up with an idea of his own, you could suggest something like:

* ★ Buy a small toy for Toys for Tots
* ★ Buy some canned goods for a canned food drive
* ★ Buy some mittens or a hat for a child in need
* ★ Give extra money in church that week

✳ **Wednesday**-Mother Teresa of Calcutta once said:

Loneliness is the most terrible poverty.

Have your child think of people who are lonely in your area. Have him pick one easy, nice thing to do, whether it be dropping off some muffins to a nursing home or stopping in for a five minute visit with a neighbor who lives alone.

✳ **Thursday**- Sit down with your entire family sometime today and decide on a Holiday Charity Project to commit to.

Depending on what groups are prevalent in your community, this may take a little or a lot of creativity.

Some ideas include:

- @ Making an entire Thanksgiving meal for a family in need
- @ Filling a box with items needed by a local food pantry
- @ Buying some gifts off a list of needed items for foster/ orphan children
- @ Donating old games or toys to a homeless shelter that accepts children.

A quick web search should do the trick, but local community papers usually contain information this time of year about charities in the area and what they are in need of as well.

✳ *Friday* This one's for you: Another timely Mother Teresa quote:

Love begins by taking care of the closest ones– the ones at home.

Courtney Loquasto

November Week 3: Inside Exercise

☀ *Monday* - Today is the day for your inside dance party! Turn on whatever music floats your boat and show your child your sweet moves from your earlier days (the *lawnmower* and *running man* absolutely count).

You can play the Freeze Game by turning off the music and having everyone freeze whatever move they are doing at that moment.

☀ *Tuesday* - Get your whistle and get ready to bark out some orders. Today is boot camp!

Have your child do:

★ Jumping jacks

★ Push-ups

★ Sit-ups

...and then march him around, following after you, chanting the Duckworth Chant cadence (the first of it's kind, which Private Willie Duckworth came up with in 1944 one night at the end of a long and tedious march, to keep the company's spirits up):

Sound-off; 1-2

Sound-off; 3-4

Cadence count

1-2-3-4;

1-2-3-4

✵ Wednesday-How's your *chi* (life energy)? It's yoga day!

Find a place in your house where your child's bare feet can stick (tile/ wood floor), or layout yoga mats if you have them. Do these simple yoga moves with him:

1. Yoga Breathing:

- ❂ Breathe in through the nose, filling up your belly first, then continue inhaling to full up your chest.
- ❂ Breathe out through the nose, emptying your chest first, then continue to exhale, emptying your belly.

- ☙ Never should you or your progeny feel any pain while breathing.
- ☙ You can explain this concept to a little-little one by telling him to take a deep, long breath in and out through his nose.

2. Mountain Pose:

- ☙ Stand with feet together, hands at sides.
- ☙ Breathe deeply and look straight ahead.
- ☙ Raise hands overhead with the inhale and lower with the exhale into:

3. Forward Bend: (from Mountain Pose, while exhaling)

- ☙ Bend at the hips and bring arms forward and down until they touch the floor.
- ☙ It's ok to bend the knees.
- ☙ Do Mountain Pose into Forward Bend several times while practicing your inhaling and exhaling.

4. The Bridge:

- Lie on your back with your knees up and hands at your sides, palms down, with feet about 6 inches apart.
- Raise your tailbone until your back is arched.
- Breathe deeply, then come down slowly and repeat.

5. The Dead Bug:

- Lie on your back, bend your knees and grab your big toes with your index and middle fingers.
- Take deep breaths and gently roll left and right.

✶ **Thursday**- Your child has been waiting for this. Let him call the shots and you become the animals he calls out.

(You may be surprised at how much exercise this actually is.)

✶ **Friday**- Ask your child which day of exercise this week was his favorite, and do that again today.

November Week 4: Thanksgiving and the Early Settlers

☀ *Monday* Tell the story of the first Thanksgiving to your child:

> Way back in 1621, 101 Puritan men, women and children spent 66 days sailing from Europe to the New World on a ship called the *Mayflower*.
>
> They were trying to go to where NYC is today, but instead had to land on what is now Cape Cod, due to strong winds.
>
> Once they were there, the settlers were helped by a Native American tribe called the *Wampanoag*.
>
> One day that Fall, the Settlers and the Native Americans had a feast to celebrate their harvest and new friendship. They ate lots of food, danced, played ball games and sang songs.

The first recorded religious Thanksgiving Day in Plymouth happened two years later in 1623, when the settlers gave thanks to God for ending a two-month drought4.

We celebrate that early feast every fourth Thursday of November with our national holiday, Thanksgiving.

※ *Tuesday*- **Interesting fact**: Many of us celebrate Thanksgiving by making and eating turkey, stuffing and pumpkin pie.

While a few pumpkins and turkey might have been on the table, the bulk of what the early settlers and Native Americans ate at their harvest celebration most likely consisted of:

★ *Deer*

★ *Corn*

★ *Eel*

★ *Shellfish*

★ *Roasted Meat and*

★ *Cranberries.*

※ *Wednesday*-What is your family thankful for? Sit down and write down your child's answers (or

---

4 From "First Thanksgiving" by Lyssa Walker, appearing in nationalgeographic.com

have him write each on individual strips of paper), and set them aside to share at tomorrow's meal.

✻ *Thursday* - Some Thanksgiving jokes:

@ If April showers bring May flowers, what do Mayflowers bring?

Pilgrims

@ What key has legs and can't open doors?

Tur-key

@ What does a turkey like to eat on Thanksgiving?

Nothing, he's stuffed

@ Why did the turkey cross the road?

To prove he wasn't chicken.

✻ *Friday* - Is there anyone who's local that would really enjoy your leftovers (sick elderly, lonely)? You've already done all of the hard work to make the meal; arranging it in a disposable container and sharing the love might be just what the Pilgrims and Wampanaogs would do!

December Week 1: Christmas Trees

✳ *Monday* - Explain that Christians (and people of other faiths, too) celebrate the season of Christmas by putting up and decorating a Christmas tree in their homes.

The traditional Christmas tree has lights and ornaments with a star or angel on top, but there are also many other variations.

Talk about what your family is going to do (or has already done) to decorate for the holidays this year. Figure out a way that your child can play an active role in your family traditions.

✳ *Tuesday* - Talk about real trees vs. artificial trees.

Some families have the same tree that they put up every year, while others pick out a new, live tree each year.

Explain that artificial trees don't need any care once they are up, while live trees must have water to stay alive (just like any other plant).

Point out the smell of fresh pine, even if it's by visiting an evergreen tree that lives outside, or by smelling fresh pine wreaths or garlands at the store.

✹ *Wednesday*-What happens to live Christmas trees after Christmas? There are several ways to recycle Christmas trees:

- Some communities will mulch your tree and give you the chippings for your yard.

- Some cities use the old trees for sand and soil erosion barriers.

- Some people sink trees into lakes as a refuge and feeding area for fish.

- Some cities have programs that use donated trees to mulch hiking trails.

✹ *Thursday*- Pick your favorite type of tree garland (construction paper chains, strung popcorn, etc.) and make one with your family.

✹ *Friday*- As it turns out, the words to "O Christmas Tree" are not:

"O Christmas Tree, O Christmas tree, dah-dot-dee-dot-dee-dot-dot."

They are:

O Christmas Tree, O Christmas Tree,

Thy leaves are so unchanging.

O Christmas Tree, O Christmas Tree

Thy leaves are so unchanging.

Not only green when summer's here,

But also when 'tis cold and drear.

O Christmas Tree, O Christmas Tree,

Thy leaves are so unchanging!

*Extra credit: See who can tell you whether a Christmas tree is deciduous or evergreen. Hint: *The answer's in the song!*

Courtney Loquasto

December Week 2: Snow

☀ *Monday* - Explain to your child that no two

snowflakes are alike. This is pretty amazing,

considering there are only 6 sides to every snowflake.

Bonus:

What is the name of a 6-sided shape?

A hexagon.

☀ *Tuesday* - Pay a little wintertime homage to what

is arguably our most famous American Christmas

song, all about a ride in the snow.

Even the tiniest toddler can shout out *hey*!

We know you've got the first verse memorized, but

how about the second? (P.S. *upsot* means

overturned):

Jingle Bells

James Pierpont (1857)

Dashing through the snow

In a one-horse open sleigh

O'er the fields we go

Laughing all the way (ha ha ha)

Bells on bobtails ring

Making spirits bright

What fun it is to laugh and sing

A sleighing song tonight

Oh, jingle bells, jingle bells

Jingle all the way

Oh what fun it is to ride

In a one horse open sleigh (Hey!)

Jingle bells, jingle bells

Jingle all the way

Oh what fun it is to ride

In a one horse open sleigh

A day or two ago

I thought I'd take a ride

And soon Miss Fanny Bright

Was seated by my side

The horse was lean and lank

Misfortune seemed his lot

We got into a drifted bank

And then we got upsot

※ **Wednesday** - Give your child a straw and a pile of cotton balls. He can blow the cotton balls all around with the straw to make his own snowstorm.

Yes, even the 8 year-old.

If you really want to take it to the next level, get out your hairdryer and give him a blizzard demonstration.

I feel I should probably mention, though, that I myself have almost set fire to/ electrocuted myself a couple of times during this exercise. My advice would be to watch the hairdryer, too (not just the cotton balls).

✳ **Thursday**- Explain that water freezes at 32 degrees Fahrenheit/ 0 degrees Celsius.

If the temperature outside is 32 degrees or below, and if it would otherwise be a rainy day, it snows. *Usually.* Two exceptions are:

1. **Sleet** is what happens when it's cold enough to snow at cloud level, but the snow passes through a warmer layer and it melts partially.

   As the melted snow passes back into freezing air, it refreezes, and becomes hard, like a pellet.

   Sleet sounds like someone saying "Shhhh" when it hits the ground.

2. **Freezing rain** is what happens when rain comes down in liquid form, but then freezes as soon as it hits anything on the earth's surface that is below freezing. We call this an ice storm.

✳ **Friday**- Tell your child about the most snow that fell in one day, which was in Anchorage, Alaska, in March 2002. 22 inches fell within 24 hours.

That's almost two feet in one day!

Ask your child how he would walk in all that snow? Take a minute to enjoy his creative answer, then talk about snowshoes, or, shoes that look like tennis rackets that are made for walking in the snow.

Courtney Loquasto

December Week 3: Good Manners

✳ *Monday* - Start the day off with one blank sheet of paper set in front of your child, along with a pack of stickers.

 For every *please* and *thank you* he offers through the day, give him a sticker to put on his sheet.

At the end of the day, if you have more than one child, the one with the most stickers wins something like an extra bedtime story. If you have one child, reward any amount over X stickers with the extra story.

✳ *Tuesday* - Ask your child to pretend that the queen is coming to share your next meal.

Try on your best British accent, (even if you end up sounding Southern instead.)

Remind your child that the queen is very polite, and that she expects everyone around her to be very polite, too.

★ What is he going to do differently when she is there?

★ What will his posture look like?

★ How will he speak?

★ How will he hold his utensils?

★ What will he do if there is only one piece of food left in the middle of the table?

★ What will he say when he is finished eating?

✳ **Wednesday**- Explain that it is very hard to hear when more than one person talks at once, interrupting included.

Decorate a plain old stick from outside and make it your family Talking Stick. Whoever has the stick gets the floor.

✳ **Thursday**- The presents are coming! Now's your chance to head off gift-exchange disasters before they occur.

Explain that everyone who is going to give your child a present thought hard about what he'd like.

Even if he isn't that fond of the present, tell him it's important for him to say **thank you** politely and to not show any disappointment.

Ask him to put himself in the shoes of the person who gave the gift. How would it make your child feel if he picked out a special gift for someone else and they said they didn't like it?

A little role-playing here might be helpful. Okay, let's call a spade a spade. It's Christmas practice.

You – "Here's a big bag of coal I picked out for you! Hope you like it!"

Your child – (*his honest response*)

You – "It would be good for you to say 'Oh, thank you very much!' Let's try that again."

✳ *Friday –* Talk about different ways to meet new people. Often it's easier for a child to introduce himself to someone else when he has a little speech prepared.

1. When a child meets an adult, he can say:

"Hello, Miss/ Mrs ____. It's nice to meet you."

Remind him to look the adult in the eye and shake hands if it's appropriate.

2. When a child meets another child, he can say:

"Hi, my name is ___. What's yours?"

And then:

"Oh, it's nice to meet you. Would you like to play on the playground with me?"

December Week 4: The Christmas Story

✧ *Monday* - Explain (or revisit) the idea that Christmas is the holiday when Christians celebrate Jesus being born.

If you have a little-little guy, you can talk about Mary being very pregnant and looking for a place to have her baby, while she and Joseph were traveling.

A nice innkeeper told them he had no space for them at the inn, but she could have the baby in the horse's stable. Mary gave birth to Jesus right there, near the animals.

If your child is older, have him tell *you the* story of Jesus being born in his own words. See how many details he remembers.

✧ *Tuesday* - Have your child help you make last minute gifts/ cards/ food for anyone that unexpectedly gave you a present this year.

✧ *Wednesday* - Decide on a new tradition to start as a family for Christmas morning. Some ideas:

★ Nobody wakes Mommy or Daddy till 8 AM
★ Make fresh OJ together
★ The oldest child gets to play Santa and pass out the gifts
★ The youngest gets to pick one toy or game the whole family must play together
★ Everyone wears J.C. birthday hats
★ The kids make breakfast.

✹ Thursday - Have your child pick out what he is wearing to church, down to the underwear, socks and shoes, even if the Christmas service isn't for five days from now.

Put the clothes in an out-of-the-way place, and bring them out when it's time to get ready for church.

This should prevent anyone from scrambling to find missing items while the rest of you freeze in the car.

That way, you can think about God during church instead of where you can find a good therapist to cure you of your outrageous Mommy/Daddy-temper.

✳ *Friday* - The holiday season is coming to an end.

Breathe, take it in, and enjoy the hard, sweaty, mood-altering amount of work you put into making this Christmas the best - Christmas - EVER!

And So, In Closing:

Well, hopefully you are feeling very satisfied with the amount of little here's and there's you've taught your little people this year! Not only did they benefit, but doesn't it feel wonderful to have all of that "common knowledge", fresh and usable, swimming around in *your* mind, too? You no longer have to avoid the conversation about US elections - you've officially been briefed. And I *dare* you to start the Horse Manure Crisis of 1894 discussion in mixed company; as unsavory a topic as it is, it does seem to interest a varied and unlikely audience!

Best of luck to you as you continue with your parenting endeavors. Don't forget to keep your book of **Little Lesson Plans** close by, and please come visit again soon - and often!

– Courtney

Courtney Loquasto

BONUS: An Easy, Free Way to Teach Your Little Ones to Read While They Still Have Their Baby Teeth

Many of us would agree that, yes, we'd like to give our child a leg-up on reading if we can, especially if there are simple, inexpensive things we can do that will get him on the right path to becoming a strong reader.

We want him to read for all sorts of logical reasons:

- It will give him independence, confidence, and a whole separate world to escape to every time he opens a book.
- It will be his foundation for learning about any topic he can dream up.
- He'll be able to soak up as much as he can stand about dinosaurs.
- He'll be able to step into an 18th century mystery in London if he wants to.
- ☆ He'll be able to entertain himself in the car without our iPhone.

So, to start - let's not over think this. There are lots and lots of good reading programs out there that work. Some are simple, some are moderately complex, some are cheap, and some are very expensive. Some incorporate animals, some incorporate kids, and one that I'm aware of utilizes a CD of an older woman's voice - rapping. (To listen to it made me thoroughly squirmy and uncomfortable, but I'm sure it works for certain kids.) Hey, who am I to judge?

My way isn't that fancy. My mom taught me how to read, and she taught me how to teach my own kids to read. She was a second-grade schoolteacher in the 60's and 70's and did some very simple things that I'd like to share with you, all of which you could start today, if you'd like.

Can't you just feel that anxiety melting away?

The Big Caveat:

I wish I could, but I cannot absolutely guarantee that this method will work for you. I am very optimistic because it's so simple and straightforward, but we won't know for sure until you try it.

Here is what we *do* know:

★ This system doesn't require you to learn anything new.
★ This system can be done while riding in your car or folding the laundry.
★ It reeks of common sense.
★ It's practically free.
★ It can work in conjunction with other reading programs your child may receive (at his preschool/ school/ tutoring center), or it can stand on its own.
★ It certainly can't *hurt* you or your kid.

Caveat-ed out? Great. Let's move on.

The one proficiency you must have in order to teach your child to read is that *you* must know how to read.

Ok, good. I don't have to point out the obvious on that one.

Also, even though you will be focusing on specific steps associated with reading skills, don't forget to continue reading age-appropriate books to your child through the whole teaching process. The more familiar he is with hearing the words in his language and how they are arranged, the easier it will be for him to read them.

Here they are- the six simple steps to reading:

1. Alphabet Song

2. Capital Letters

3. Letter Sounds

4. Sound Out Words

5. Lower Case Letters

6. Read!

Step 1: Teach Him the "The Alphabet Song".

(Yep, the one that sounds like "Twinkle, Twinkle").

Really commit to it, which means singing it to your child about four times a day until he can sing it himself. You may very well grow to resent this song deeply, but it will help with the next steps.

Once he can sing it on his own,

Step 2: Teach Him What Each Letter Looks Like.

All of the capital letters first.

Some reading experts suggest teaching little ones the lowercase letters first, since the huge majority of printed words consist mostly of lowercase letters. The problem is, lowercase *b* and *d* and *p* and *q* look a lot alike, since they are basically mirror images of each other. You don't have that problem with the uppercase letters, which is why I've found it easier to teach those, first.

And how do you actually sit and teach your child what each letter looks like? Well, you can point them out in everyday things (like alphabet soup), on billboards, in books, magnets, etc., but you are probably going to also want a standard set of letters to use over and over again so the child can get very familiar with each letter.

Yes, I'm talking about flashcards.

Flashcards:

There are oodles of alphabet flash cards for sale out there. Many are bright, colorful cards with the capital letter, lowercase letter, and a picture, all jammed into one spot.

All of that excitement on one card seems like a lot to process, even for an adult brain. How's a kid supposed to learn what the letter *X* looks like when it's sitting there next to a picture of a skeleton, as seen through an X-ray?

We tried this at my house. My kids had nightmares about the skeleton and completely forgot which letter was associated with it.

But, we've always had a lot of luck with plain old, black-and-white flashcards.

My former-schoolteacher mother is very stressed-out that I am suggesting you teach your children the letters with flashcards that do not have pictures on them. She was trained to teach picture/ letter / sound association and remembers her students learning their letters much easier when there was a picture to go with it.

In doing some research as to whether or not we have empirical data to settle the matter, we do. It says we're both right! For every study that says pictures help kids use different parts of their brains to better learn a letter, there's another study that says the pictures cause the child to remember the picture, not the letter.

And even as I write this, I notice my 6 year-old has drawn pictures on the back of my plain flashcards, which my 2 year old flips over to see. And he's memorized which letter goes with which picture. Oh well.

You be the judge! You have to make decisions like this for your family all the time anyway. I just figured I'd give you my two cents so that you have another data point to consider when deciding for yourself.

Though, I did get a *little* presumptuous and included black and white, straightforward letter flashcards after this chapter (one uppercase set and one lowercase set). I couldn't easily find a plain-old set anywhere when I looked to buy them for myself, so I thought I'd include them for you in case you were interested. You can also print them up at SimpleFamilyJoys.com

If you want the brightly-colored flashcards with pictures, you'll have to go to Target. My feelings won't be hurt! Whatever works for your kid is the right answer. (Maybe your 6 year-old can draw some pictures on yours, too.)

And...GO!

When you're ready to begin teaching, start with just **one capital letter**, until he memorizes that letter. It could take a week or more for him to recognize that letter on his own. You don't have to go in the order of the alphabet, especially since some of the letters are easier to teach than the others. For example, *O* is a fun one - your mouth makes that shape when you say it.

You can say words that mean something special to him when you show him each letter, like "D, Daddy!" Or "M, Mommy!", in order to help him remember which is which. See? I'm not totally unreasonable or against all word / letter associations.

Once he's confident with that one letter, move on to the next letter. At the end of each lesson, make sure you circle back and review the letters he's already learned.

This step could take a few months or more, but keep doing it until your child remembers all or most of the letters of the alphabet.

Step 3: Teach Him What Sound(s) Each Letter Makes.

Grab those flashcards again, and, in the same way you taught him which letter is which, teach him what sounds each makes. Don't forget, some letters make more than one sound (for example, *A* says *aeh* and *ay*).

Only work on one or two letters at a time, until he remembers on his own what sound(s) each make(s). Circle back and review the previously learned sounds at the end of each session.

Do this until he has a good grasp of most of the letter sounds of the alphabet.

You can do this throughout the day, as you see letters out in the world together.

"See that big C on that sign? C says 'kuh' and 'sss'. What does A say?"

Here's your reminder for what sounds each letter makes:

A-   "aeh" and "ay"

B-   "buh"

C-   "kuh" and "sss"

D-   "duh"

E-   "eh" and "ee"

F-   "fuh"

G-   "guh" and "juh"

H-   "huh"

I-   "ih" and "eye"

J-   "juh"

K-   "kuh"

L-   "LLL"

M-   "mmm"

N-   "nnn"

O-   "ah" and "oh"

P-   "puh"

Q-   "kwa"

R-   "er"

S-   "sss"

T-   "tuh"

U-   "uh" and "you"

V-   "vuh"

W-   "wuh"

X-   "cks"

Y-   "yuh" and "ee"

Z-   "zzz"

Step 4: Show Him How to Sound Out Small Words.

Sounding out a word - even if it takes 15 minutes per 3 letter word - counts as reading! Yay and yippee for you and he!

Oh, but remember your patience, here, Grasshopper. Like…of Job. This step might take a while.

Show Him How it's Done:

1. If you haven't done so already, tear out the uppercase flashcards from the back of this book (or, to save your book, print them out at SimpleFamilyJoys.com).

2. Arrange the flashcards into a small, easy word like

"CAT"

3. Show him how to sound out the word, by *very slowly* pointing to each letter and sounding it out as you go:

C says "cuh"

A says "aeh"

T says "tuh"

4. Then, SLOWLY, say just the sounds as you point to each letter:

"CCCCCC-AAAAAAA-TTTTTTTT"

5. Now a little faster:

"CCC-AAA-TTT"

6. Now faster:

"CCAATT".

7. Now normal speed:

"CAT. CAT. See? CAT. Now you try it!"

Now, go through those very same steps for another simple, 3 letter word, like SUN or SIT or RUN.

Do it again and again until he loses interest, and then try to have him sound out the same simple 3 or 4 letter words the next day. (Remember all of the Sesame Street characters that sounded out words for us through the years? Channel 30% of their enthusiasm for phonics and you're golden.)

Maybe he won't get it right away. Maybe it will take a day or week or month for him to do it himself. Keep showing him how it's done, though, and he'll eventually get it.

On the day he gets it, you can jump up and down, do a cartwheel and mark it down in his baby book as the very first day he learned to read all by himself!

Reinforcements:

There are some targeted TV shows that focus on the very reading skills you are teaching in this step. Here are a few to try:

- ★ Super Y
- ★ Word Girl
- ★ Word World
- ★ Sesame Street

Also, when you are reading books to him during this stage, look closely for words in all caps in the story and pictures that he can try to sound out by himself. Point out STOP signs and TAXI cabs and CVS stores when you're out.

The world of print is slowly starting to come into focus all around him at this point, and it is truly fascinating to witness as his parent.

Step 5: Teach Him the Lower Case Letters.

Now that he's familiar with the all of the letters of the alphabet and the sounds that each make, it's time to introduce him to the "little letters".

You can now either rip out the lowercase flashcards in the end of this book, or print them at SimpleFamilyJoys.com.

Use the same method you did for the uppercase letters (focusing on **just one letter** until your child memorizes it) and remember to review all of the letters he's already learned at the end of each lesson.

This step should take less time than it did to teach him the capital letters, but, remember: You are introducing 26 new symbols to your child. One...at...a...time. It's still going to take a while. You may want to get comfortable.

And remember, be prepared to spend extra time on *b* and *d* as well as *p* and *q*. Hopefully you'll be happy you taught the capital letters first. These four little mirror-images are tricky!

Step 6: Read, Read, Read!

You've done it! Congratulations to you both! You have him able to sound out words on his own. He's not great at it yet, but he's on his way. Now it's time to have him read as much as he can, as often as you can sit with him (to make sure he's able to keep moving along.)

You might want to have him try to read very, very easy books at first, in order to build his confidence. Hooked on Phonics' easy reader **Hop Books** for Kindergarten (try eBay) and **My First BOB Books** were specifically designed to be the some of the very first books a child can read on his own.

You can also look for books that have:

★ *"Step into Reading, Step 1"*

★ *"I Can Read - Level 1"*, *or*

★ *"Level 1"*

on the cover, but you may want to flip through the pages to make sure they are filled with easy 3 and 4 letter words.

Next he can try to read some of the more challenging easy-reader books, like **Hop on Pop** by Dr. Seuss, or **Are You My Mother** by P.D. Eastman, for example.

There's a lot more ahead for him to learn about the English language: long sounds versus short sounds, silent **e**'s, sight words that don't really follow the rules, special phonics criteria that only apply some of the time, grammar, punctuation, sentence structure and more.

But don't worry - he'll get there.

Once he can read out loud, you can gently correct him when he gets stuck or pronounces a word incorrectly. Every time you do, you're actually giving him an informal, mini-English lesson. His mind is constantly indexing rules about how the world works, your corrections included. Even though you're not categorically teaching him all of the rules to the English language, you're at least demonstrating many of them in action.

Plus, you don't want to take *all* of the fun away from his schoolteachers. You've gotta leave some of the glory for Mrs. Crabapple!

And one last idea: When you're reading books *to* him at this stage, you can point to the words as you're reading them. That way, he can see what the words look like as he hears them, and he may very well start to recognize some of those words (which will serve as another confidence booster for him).

Ok, so to review what we've learned, what are our 6 steps to reading fantastic-ness, again?

1. Alphabet Song

2. Capital Letters

3. Letter Sounds

4. Sound Out Words

5. Lower Case Letters

6. Read!

That's it! Easy-peasy lemon squeezy, (as our local 6-year-old set says). And all that it cost you was the price of this book, which you probably bought for the Little Lesson Plans, anyway.

"The more that you read, the more things you will know. The more you learn, the more places you'll go."

— Dr. Seuss, "I Can Read With My Eyes Shut!"

The

_____

Family's
Stodgy, Old-School,
Alphabet
Flashcards.
That's Right - With No
Pictures.

Courtney Loquasto

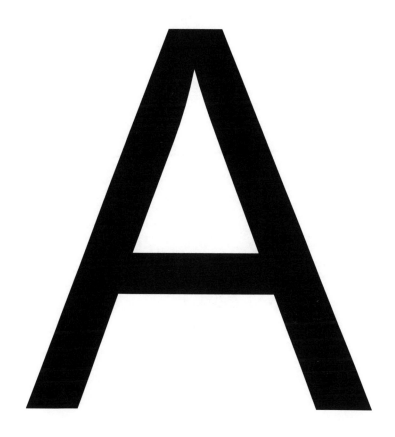

Courtney Loquasto

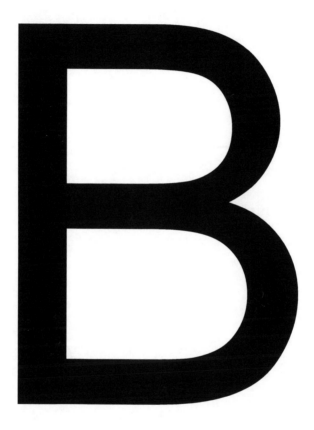

Courtney Loquasto

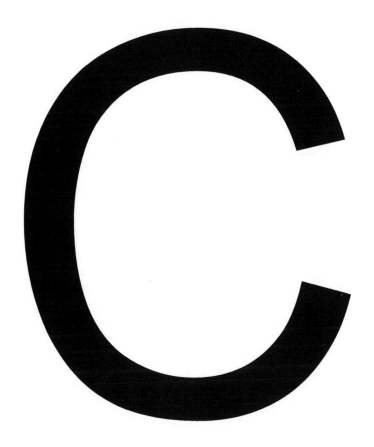

Courtney Loquasto

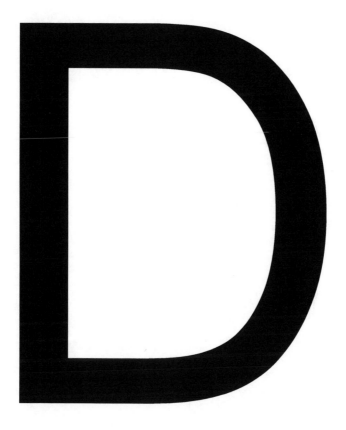

Courtney Loquasto

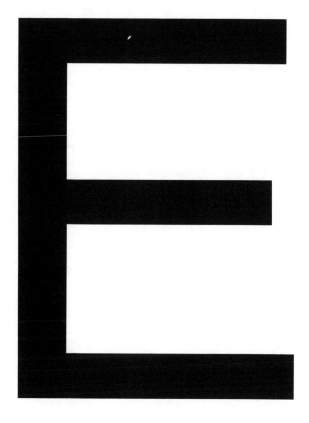

Courtney Loquasto

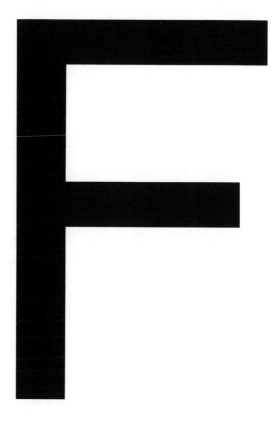

Courtney Loquasto

Courtney Loquasto

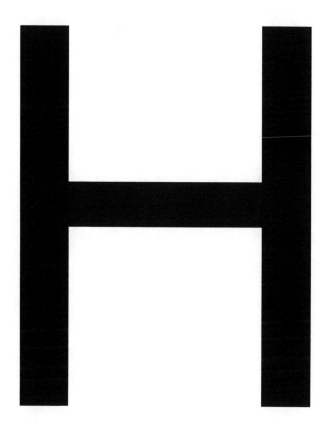

Courtney Loquasto

Courtney Loquasto

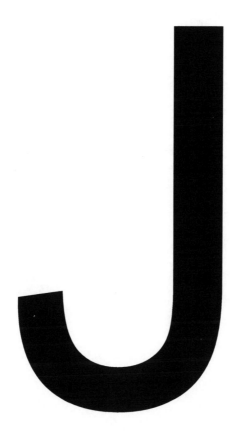

Courtney Loquasto

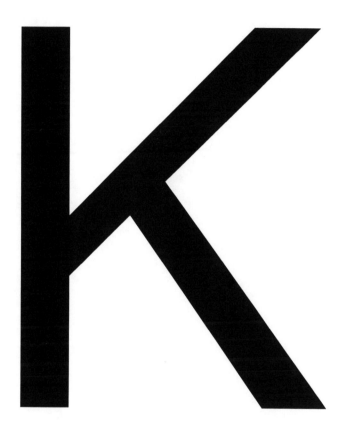

Courtney Loquasto

Courtney Loquasto

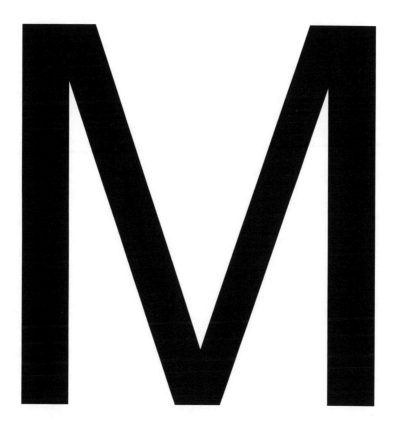

Courtney Loquasto

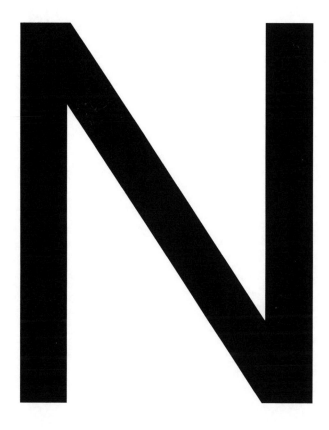

Courtney Loquasto

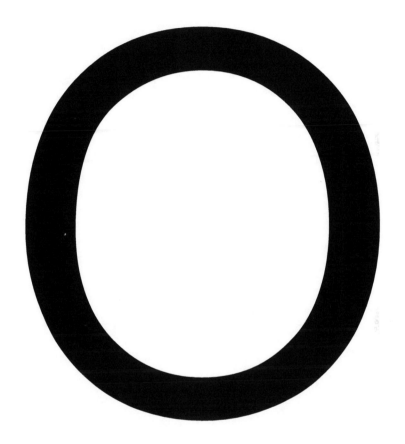

Courtney Loquasto

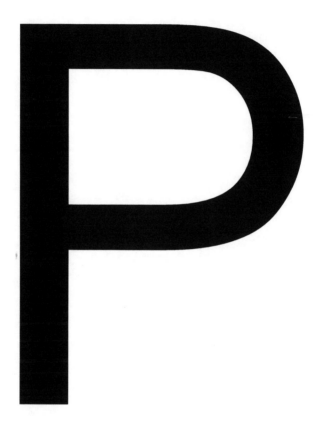

Courtney Loquasto

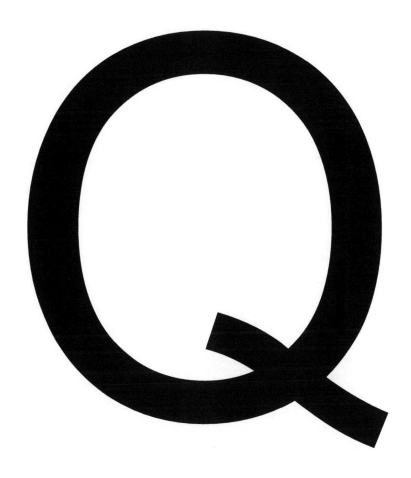

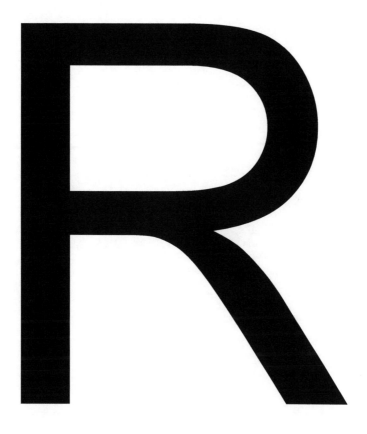

Courtney Loquasto

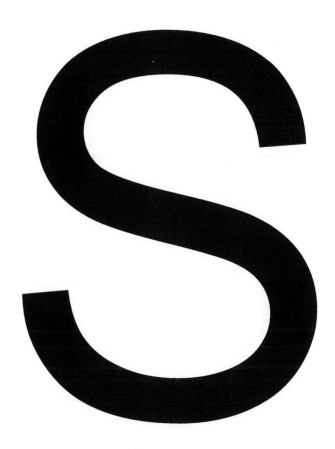

Courtney Loquasto

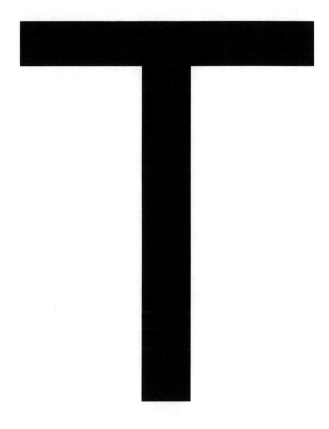

Courtney Loquasto

Courtney Loquasto

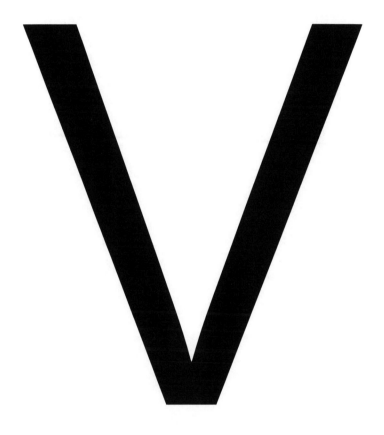

Courtney Loquasto

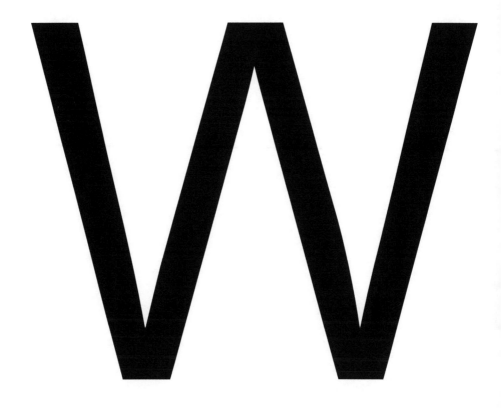

Courtney Loquasto

Courtney Loquasto

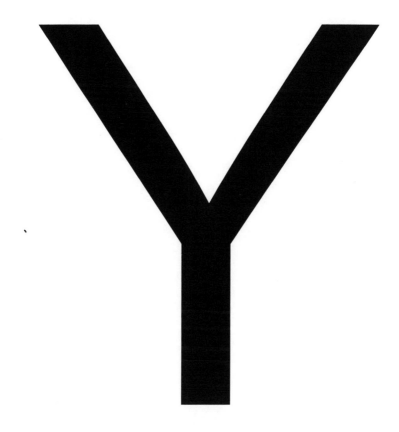

Courtney Loquasto

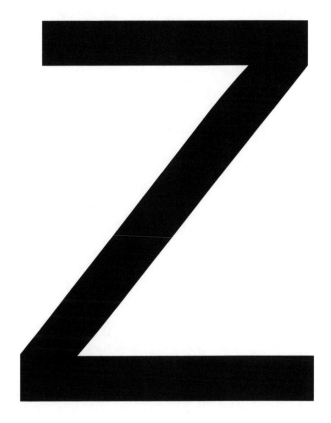

Courtney Loquasto

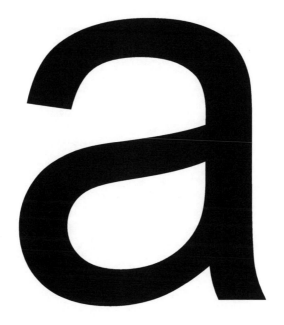

Courtney Loquasto

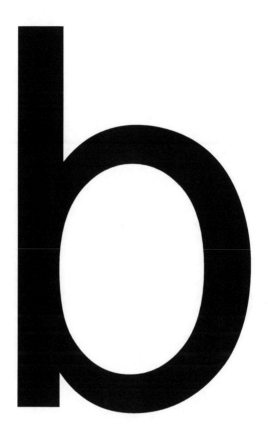

Courtney Loquasto

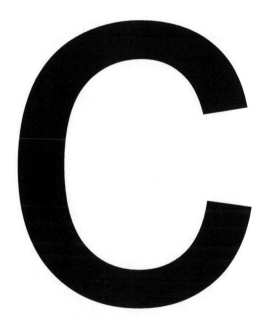

Courtney Loquasto

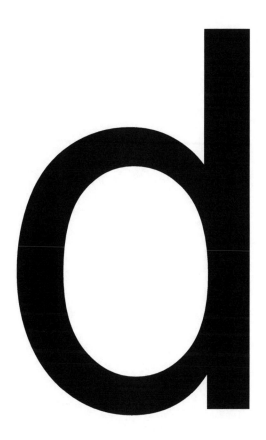

Courtney Loquasto

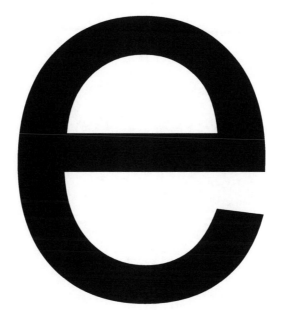

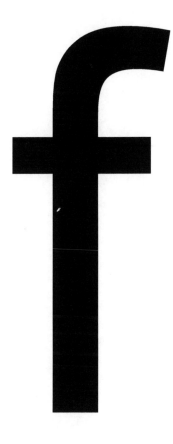

Courtney Loquasto

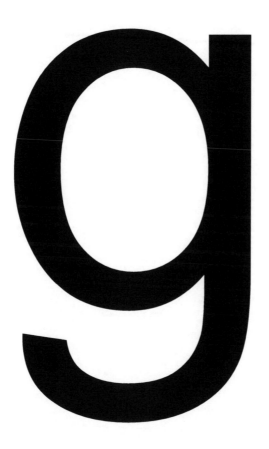

Courtney Loquasto

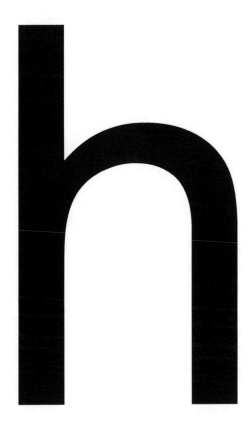

Courtney Loquasto

Courtney Loquasto

Courtney Loquasto

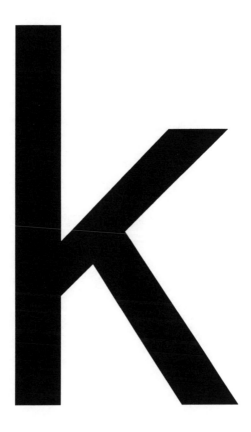

Courtney Loquasto

Courtney Loquasto

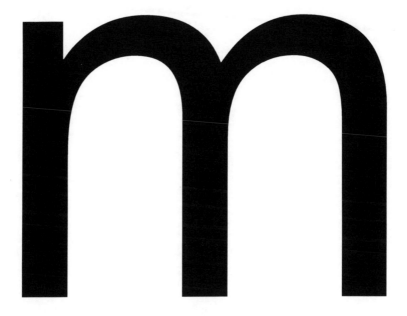

Courtney Loquasto

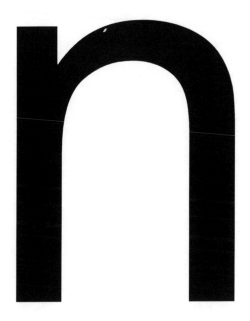

Courtney Loquasto

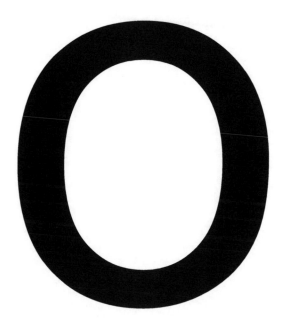

Courtney Loquasto

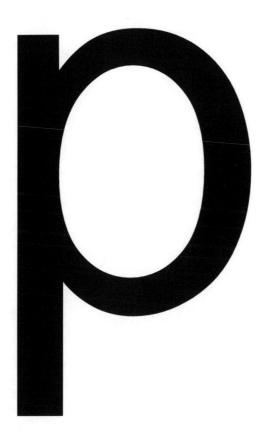

Courtney Loquasto

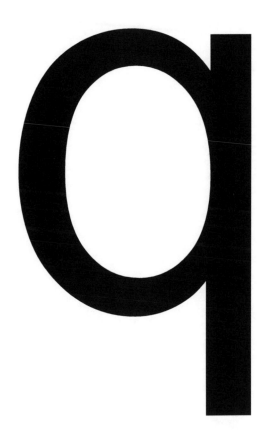

Courtney Loquasto

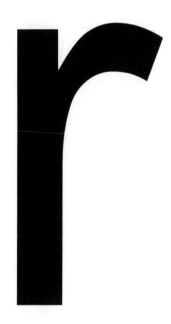

Courtney Loquasto

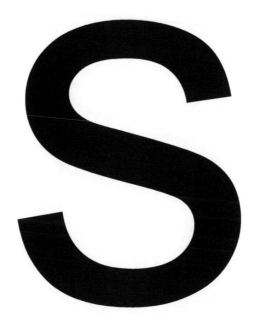

Courtney Loquasto

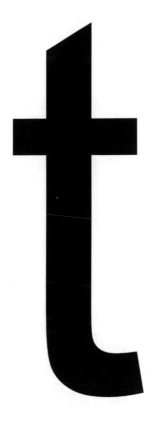

Courtney Loquasto

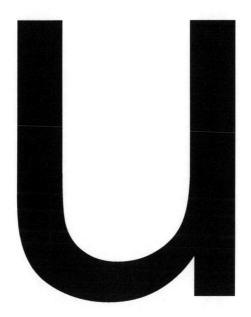

Courtney Loquasto

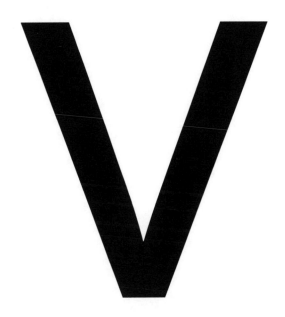

Courtney Loquasto

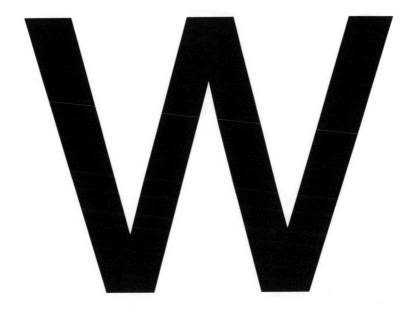

Courtney Loquasto

Courtney Loquasto

Courtney Loquasto

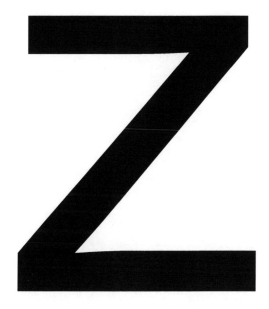

Courtney Loquasto

About the Author

Before the first of her three children was born, Courtney managed a team of project managers and process experts for a Fortune 10 company. She's spent the last four years adapting successful business tools for use in the home. She's taught Family Strategy Development to at-risk pregnant women, and consults small businesses on how to make their processes more efficient. She lives with her husband and children near Atlanta, where lots of Candyland-ing and freeze-tagging takes place.

Watch for more in the YEAR of LITTLE LESSON PLANS series coming soon!

SimpleFamilyJoys.com

eBook available on Amazon.com

Made in the USA
Lexington, KY
30 June 2013

ABOUT THE AUTHOR BY JAX NUNNERLEY

I first met Howard when interviewing him for a job. I can still remember that he was dressed in an open-neck shirt, trousers, and what became to be his trademark waistcoat—not exactly interview dress. He had the technical experience that was required, but the main thing that stuck in my mind was his personality. He was the type of person who had always used his personality to get what he wanted, and I felt that his technical ability was secondary. His personality can only be described as "cheeky." Despite this he was offered the job and proved to be a very dedicated and knowledgeable employee. Over a time we became friends, and I found him to have a terrific sense of humour, rarely letting things get him down but never showing any serious side (except when it came to his work), even to the point of being unsympathetic at times. His "cheek" was always bubbling on the surface,